By the same author:
Allergies
Arthritis
Menopause
Stress
Weight Control

ECZEMA AND PSORIASIS
HOW YOUR DIET CAN HELP

Stephen Terrass

Thorsons
An Imprint of HarperCollinsPublishers

To Nicola, whose love, understanding, patience,
encouragement and valuable input have helped me
immeasurably in the writing of this book

Thorsons
An Imprint of HarperCollins*Publishers*
77–85 Fulham Palace Road,
Hammersmith, London W6 8JB
1160 Battery Street
San Francisco, California 94111–1213

Published by Thorsons 1995

10 9 8 7 6 5 4 3

A catalogue record for this book
is available from the British Library

ISBN 0 7225 3148 6

Printed and bound in Great Britain by
Caledonian International Book Manufacturing Ltd, Glasgow

CONTENTS

ACKNOWLEDGEMENTS

The author wishes to thank the following for their valuable support and assistance in this project: Richard Passwater PhD for his inspiration and reviewing of the manuscript; editor Wanda Whiteley and copy-editor Barbara Vesey; Eileen Campbell and Jane Graham-Maw for their help and commitment to this series; Geoff Duffield, Megan Slyfield, Michele Turney and Sarah Sutton for their hard work and dedication; special thanks to Rand Skolnick, John Steenson, Cheryl Thallon, Leyanne Scharff and Fay Higginbotham for their valuable support; Nibs Laskor for his generosity; and all my friends from health food stores and colleagues in the natural medicine field. Most of all, fondest thanks to Nicola Squire and Shirley Terrass for their love and encouragement.

The dietary and health recommendations in this book are meant only as guidelines. Neither the author nor the publishers can assume responsibility if any of the dietary or lifestyle recommendations in this book do not have the desired effect. Please consult a qualified health practitioner before embarking on any new diet or health regime.

Eczema and psoriasis are more than skin disorders. As a youth, I remember hearing the advertisements for a cream to treat 'the heartbreak of psoriasis'. As a nutrition researcher, I am also involved in a good deal of health education. After lectures I have had discussions with many people suffering from the heartbreak of psoriasis and have found that it needlessly hampers their social life. Sufferers often feel disfigured and shy away from others, whereas the people they are avoiding hardly notice the condition and pay no attention to it. Yet the sufferers continue to have emotional or psychological problems which serve only to worsen the condition. A vicious cycle is formed: more emotional stress followed by still worsening of the condition, and the cycle turns again.

Eczema and psoriasis are more than skin disorders in that they psychologically affect social behaviour, but more than that, these two disorders are indeed physically more than skin disorders. As nutrition expert Stephen Terrass points out, there are many factors involved in both of these skin disorders and they reflect conditions beyond the skin. Thus, control of these disorders also requires going beyond the skin itself. Conventional medicine is usually preoccupied with treating the symptoms with creams, lotions and steroids. The steroids are intended to reduce the inflammation that is common to both disorders.

However, Stephen Terrass has researched the scientific literature and found that several natural inflammation fighters have greater advantages and that many sufferers respond well to simple dietary changes. There is considerable evidence that one's diet plays a very important role in both disorders – the proper diet will alleviate the inflammation due to sensitivities to certain foods, while the wrong eating habits will increase the inflammation common to both disorders.

Through many years of experience of helping people through his nutritional education lectures, Stephen Terrass has tested the published scientific findings and clearly explains how the reader can determine which diet and which nutritional and/or herbal aids would work for each individual. Stephen Terrass presents clear explanations in an interesting and educational manner. One way to reduce the stress that exacerbates the inflammation common to both disorders is to read this book.

Richard A. Passwater, PhD
Berlin, MD, USA
13 January, 1995

When we think of our health, we tend to concentrate on the major organs such as the heart, liver, lungs and so on. With this emphasis on the more obvious body parts, we often overlook other areas which may also be of considerable importance to our overall state of physical wellbeing.

It may come as a surprise, but the skin is actually the largest organ of the human body. By definition, this means it serves an essential function maintaining our health. We often take it for granted, thinking that it is there 'just to hold the bones and muscles in place', or perhaps to protect us from the outside environment – but its abilities go much further.

We do pay some attention to our skin, but more out of vanity than anything else. We hate getting acne when we are younger, and hate getting wrinkles when we are older. There is certainly nothing wrong with wanting to look good; the problem stems from not being aware of the fact that the condition of our skin can tell us a great deal about what is going on in the other parts of our bodies.

There is no better example of this than in the case of eczema and psoriasis. While these conditions are not the same, there are some common principles which apply to both. Perhaps the most important is that, while they are both skin disorders, neither is exclusively a problem of the skin itself. Eczema and psoriasis represent unique and multifaceted malfunctions within several different systems of the body.

The similarities between eczema and psoriasis mean each is often mistaken for the other. This can be a major problem, as the causes of each are in many ways quite different, as is the most appropriate mode of treatment for each one.

The fact that the source of eczema and psoriasis is not merely 'skin deep' makes the standard medical treatments largely limited in effect, as they tend to concentrate on the skin and treat only the symptoms. They also typically cause side-effects.

The purpose of this book is first to explain the two conditions – their symptoms and causes as well as how to distinguish between them. Secondly, we will look at the mechanics behind the conditions and the malfunctions within the body which give rise to the symptoms and their underlying causes. Following this, the kinds of foods which can help or hurt sufferers will be covered. Finally, we will discuss the natural treatment measures appropriate to eczema and psoriasis, including vitamin and mineral therapy, herbal medicine and other nutritional substances. This information will examine very safe methods based on published scientific and medical research.

Both eczema and psoriasis are indeed very uncomfortable to the sufferer, both physically and emotionally. At their worst they can be physically debilitating and painful, and even the mildest cases can cause great inconvenience and may well worsen as time goes on if nothing is done to stop the progress of the condition.

Whether a sufferer is in too much pain to put on clothing, or just has a mild patch here and there, it is important to understand the safest and most effective approaches that can bring relief. Fortunately there is evidence to suggest that many safe and natural treatments will benefit not only the symptoms but also the causes of eczema and psoriasis. With the help all of nature has to offer, the potential for a life free from eczema or psoriasis may be in your grasp!

PART 1

Definitions

CHAPTER 1

What Is Eczema?

Although both eczema and psoriasis are often discussed in conjunction with one another, there really is a great deal of difference between them in terms of both their symptoms and their likely causes. In this chapter we will look into the background and definition of eczema as well as its common symptoms, in order to make it easier to identify and distinguish it from other skin disorders.

Eczema is an inflammatory skin condition which generally manifests as red, itchy patches and sometimes weeping blisters on various parts of the body. Eczema is sometimes classified as *atopic dermatitis*. (The term atopic refers to *atopy*, which means a tendency to develop health disorders associated with allergies.) The fact that it is both an atopic disorder and an inflammatory condition is quite significant, as we will look into shortly.

Although it is not as well known a condition as, for example, acne, it is more common than you might think. It has been suggested that it affects between 2½ and 7 per cent of the population. Oddly enough, eczema appears to be most common in infants, and it is quite common for an infant with eczema to develop asthma later on in childhood. This association will be discussed in more detail in Chapter 4. Nevertheless, there are many adults who suffer with eczema, both those who had it in childhood and many who developed it only later, in adulthood.

As with many health disorders, eczema is not a one-dimensional condition and there is no single direct cause for the problem in every sufferer. There is, however, plenty of research to point to the fact that there are a few major malfunctions which can cause and/or exacerbate eczema. The majority of the research does strongly point to a very common association with allergies, particularly to various foods. This is an association which we will delve into in some detail in Chapter 4.

COMMON SYMPTOMS

Eczema has various classic characteristics which help to identify and differentiate it from other skin disorders. Usually sufferers will develop all associated symptoms, and all will have most symptoms, to varying degrees of severity.

RED, INFLAMED LESIONS
The parts of the skin affected by eczema develop lesions which will often appear as patches, blisters and/or scratches. The more severe the lesions, the redder they will appear. Eventually, the blistering which may occur can begin to weep fluid.

SEVERE ITCHING
Generally, the area or areas affected by eczema lesions are very itchy and uncomfortable. The itching will fluctuate in some sufferers from being quite severe at times to more or less unnoticeable at others. In other sufferers, the itching can be either consistently mild or severe. The severity of the itching will change based on how active the eczema is

at the time. Naturally, this symptom will sometimes produce an overwhelming urge to scratch, which will, not surprisingly, make matters worse.

THICKENING OF THE SKIN

The skin in the affected areas will typically become abnormally thick. This thickening can be brought about through trauma to the patches from scratching, rubbing, etc.

SKIN DRYNESS

The affected areas will typically be rather dry in comparison to unaffected areas. The skin in these parts is less able to hold water than normal skin.

Areas Affected

Although eczema can occur in many parts of the body, there are some areas where it is particularly common. These include:

- the face
- elbows
- behind the knees
- wrists.

No place is a good place to have eczema, and each area has its own special disadvantages. When the problem is very evident on the face, one suffers not only physical discomfort but naturally can often experience emotional or psychological difficulties as well. The psychological stress eczema can cause may only make matters worse and may actually cause a flare-up of the physical symptoms. When the problem exists in areas normally covered by clothing, the consolation of having 'hidden' lesions is often offset by the fact that wearing clothes over them makes them most uncomfortable.

As eczema is classified as an inflammatory condition, in order to understand eczema and what causes its symptoms, it is important to first look at the process of inflammation and how and why it occurs (see Chapter 3).

CHAPTER 2

What Is Psoriasis?

Psoriasis is a relatively common skin condition which has very unusual causes and symptoms. In can manifest in more than one way and can affect many different parts of the body.

In general, psoriasis is manifested by an abnormal scaling of the skin over well-delineated reddish patches. Psoriasis can occur in various parts of the body although the most common areas to be affected are the scalp, face and certain parts of the limbs.

Psoriasis, like eczema, occurs more frequently than you might expect. It is thought to affect approximately 3 per cent of the population and, also like eczema, there is a very high tendency (about half of the cases) for the condition to be shared among blood relatives. As will be mentioned in Chapter 4, the family connection in eczema can be traced, to a great extent, to common allergic tendencies among family members. The reason for the familial link in the case of psoriasis is not as clear, but there are some possible connections which will be discussed later.

Psoriasis is the perfect example of how a malfunction of many different processes in the body can manifest most noticeably on the skin. The possible causes of this multi-faceted condition are many, and probably many different factors are involved even in individual cases. In Chapter 5 we will look into this in some detail, particularly concentrating not only on the skin itself, but on dysfunction of the liver, improper digestion and the effects of harmful bacteria.

COMMON SYMPTOMS

As there are some similarities between psoriasis and other skin disorders, it may be helpful to elaborate on the common symptom patterns in order to aid proper identification.

SCALING OF THE SKIN

Over the top of psoriatic skin lesions there will be a characteristic build-up of silvery scales. The quantity of these excessive skin cells will fluctuate with the severity of the condition. While the sufferer may feel the urge to remove these scales, doing so often irritates the tissue underneath and also reveals the reddened, inflamed patch of skin below.

RED, INFLAMED PATCHES OR RASH

The tissue underneath the scales is generally irritated and red and is very susceptible to further damage when the sufferer rubs the area or picks at the scales. These patches are generally very sharply delineated and may itch and feel unduly warm, especially during a worsening of the condition.

Areas Affected

Psoriasis can affect the skin in many areas of the body, particularly skin which has been weakened in some way such as due to repeated stress (e.g. rubbing, scratching).

The following are some of the most common parts affected:

- the scalp (may start out appearing like normal dandruff)
- wrists
- ankles
- elbows
- knees
- face.

In spite of the fact that psoriasis is manifested in the skin, there are strong associations with other tissues of the body as well. In many sufferers there seems to be a link between psoriasis and the development of arthritis (inflammation of the joints). If you suffer with arthritis I recommend that you read my book *Arthritis* (Thorsons, 1994).

The nail tissue can also be affected by psoriasis, which causes the surface of the nail to have a stippled texture. This too will fluctuate depending on the severity of the psoriasis.

Understanding the symptoms of psoriasis is important both from the standpoint of proper identification as well as treatment; however, as with all health disorders, this should not cause you to disregard the underlying causes. In fact this is especially true of psoriasis, which is a multi-faceted disorder. As a result, there are many different angles to be addressed for the best chance of successful prevention and treatment. This will be covered in depth in Chapter 5.

PART II

Development

While it is only natural that sufferers will be most concerned with treating the symptoms of eczema or psoriasis, there are some very strong reasons why identifying the underlying causes should be given prime consideration.

1. Not addressing the cause of any disorder means continually having to suppress the symptoms rather than putting an end to them once and for all. Treating only the symptoms does nothing to make the condition go away.
2. Many symptomatic treatments, at least as far as drugs are concerned, can have significant side-effects, especially if used over the long term. In many cases their benefits frequently begin to wane over time, unless the dosage is increased – which, of course, can lead to further problems.
3. In the case of eczema or psoriasis, the primary causes of the main symptoms can have damaging effects on other parts or functions of the body as well. Treating the symptoms on the skin, for instance, will often not benefit the other areas affected by the underlying cause – sometimes, the treatments can actually weaken other areas or body functions.
4. Correcting the cause will have general benefits to your overall state of health; ignoring the cause will do just the opposite.

Before we look (in Chapters 4 and 5) at the primary causes of eczema and psoriasis, we will first analyse *inflammation*, which triggers many of the most obvious symptoms of these two conditions.

CHAPTER 3

Inflammation in Skin Disorders

INFLAMMATION

In terms of symptoms, it is the inflammation of eczema that is particularly damaging. The same is true for the more severe cases of psoriasis.

A typical medical definition for inflammation suggests that it is generally characterized by the following symptoms:

- local swelling
- pain and/or tenderness
- redness
- discernible warmth.

Of course, this is the pattern of symptoms that is so familiar to us when we think about arthritis; especially the swelling and pain. Actually, inflammation can occur in many tissues of the body when they have become injured or damaged in some way, or if they are infected by a foreign substance such as a virus or harmful bacteria. The manner in which inflammation manifests itself will depend greatly on the tissues involved, as well as on the type of condition the person is suffering with.

The inflammatory process itself (and its symptoms) are basically the same regardless of the type of condition;

however, it is what occurs *prior to* the inflammatory reaction that can vary greatly.

CAUSES OF INFLAMMATORY SYMPTOMS

As with all the processes in the body, inflammation doesn't just happen; there is a rather complex and confusing chemical process which produces inflammation and its symptoms. This process highlights one of the aspects of inflammation that many find difficult to accept – that it is a normal and required process in the body.

The process of inflammation generally occurs in the following manner and for the following reasons:

- Any local swelling occurs when the tiny capillaries in the affected area become more permeable. What this means is that they allow certain things to pass through them more readily than would typically be the case. In inflammation, that which is allowed to pass through more easily includes various components of the body's immune system.
- The redness and warmth in the affected area is generally produced by the increased blood flow to the area. This increased blood flow allows substances responsible for repair of the damaged area to circulate there more quickly.
- The pain or irritation can be linked to the swelling and heat, but a certain inflammatory chemical called *histamine* can stimulate 'pain fibres' in the area affected by the inflammation. As the condition worsens, the local nerves will be substantially irritated, causing chronic discomfort. It is typically a combination of these factors which is involved.

The Mast Cells

The process of inflammation is initiated by a certain type of cell in the body, called the *mast cell*. Oddly enough, the mast cells are members of the natural defence system of our bodies, the immune system. Among other things, the primary function of the immune system is actually to protect the body from harmful bacteria, viruses, cancer cells, and anything identified as an 'invader' by the body.

The main components of the immune system are called *white blood cells*. There are many types of white blood cells, and each has its own functions. Mast cells are just one of the types of white blood cells, but instead of being directly involved in attacking invaders, they are responsible for the main chemical processes involved in inflammation. While other white blood cells patrol the body looking for invaders, the mast cells locate themselves along blood vessels in the tissues and wait for some sort of tissue damage.

How does a mast cell cause all of this horrible and agonizing inflammation?

a) by triggering the release of *histamine* locally in the tissues
b) by causing the release of *leukotrienes*
c) by activating inflammatory *prostaglandins*
d) by causing reactions that lead to *chemotaxis* (chemotaxis is a process whereby mast cell-derived chemicals attract 'attacking' white blood cells to the affected area).

HISTAMINE

Histamine may already be familiar to you. We usually think about it in terms of allergies, as an *anti*-histamine is often used to suppress an allergic reaction. Anti-histamines work because it is histamine which primarily produces the allergic symptoms in the first place. Allergic symptoms, too, are the result of inflammation.

Histamine and related chemicals account directly for the redness, warmth and pain or irritation of eczema or psoriasis.

LEUKOTRIENES

Leukotrienes make up another type of inflammatory chemical; they are particularly worrying as they can be more than a thousand times more inflammatory than histamine. Leukotrienes, also triggered by mast cells, are very important to the healing process and can account for much of the pain and irritation felt in the affected area of skin. Leukotrienes are created from *fatty acids* derived from dietary fats. The specific type of fatty acid responsible for the inflammatory leukotrienes is *arachidonic acid*. Within the diet, arachidonic acid is found in animal fats. Leukotrienes are created when this fatty acid is exposed to oxygen in the body.

PROSTAGLANDINS

Prostaglandins are another class of inflammatory substances, involved in the activation of inflammation and aiding the effects of chemicals such as histamine. Prostaglandins are hormone-like substances which, like leukotrienes, are made from the metabolism of dietary fats. Actually, prostaglandins can either increase or decrease inflammation, depending on the type involved. The one most responsible for causing inflammation is called *prostaglandin E2 (PGE2)*.

Arachidonic acid is held in storage in the body until an 'emergency' occurs, such as tissue damage (e.g. as seen in eczema or psoriasis) or infection (very common in eczema-affected areas), where it is then converted into PGE2 to produce an inflammatory response.

BENEFITS OF INFLAMMATION

In spite of the fact that the mast cell-induced inflammation sounds very negative and harmful, it is, in fact, a natural and necessary response for maintaining health and for the body's protection and repair:

1. The dilation of blood vessels (redness and warmth), increased capillary permeability (local swelling) and chemotaxis all promote the circulation of 'invader-destroying' white blood cells into the affected area – which, among other things, help clear up debris from damaged cells and eliminate harmful bacteria.
2. The pain activation and irritation provide obvious warning signals that tissue damage has occurred, and help deter us from further injuring the area with unnecessary physical contact. This allows healing or repair to take place more quickly.

Although histamine, leukotrienes and PGE2 cause much of what we deem to be negative about inflammation, if the inflammatory process did not exist, the body could not carry out even the simplest healing process, nor would we know that there was anything wrong, until it was perhaps too late.

As these inflammatory chemicals are manufactured from dietary sources, it is clear that we do have some control over their production. As it turns out, there is vast scientific proof that we have a great deal of control over their levels in the body, and later in the book

(Chapters 6–9) we will look at measures which can be utilized to decrease their production without damaging the body's natural healing processes. Clearly, manipulating the supply of these chemicals would have a considerable effect on inflammation and thus on the symptoms of both eczema and psoriasis. Studies seem to suggest that an increased release of histamine from mast cells is the most prominent inflammatory factor in eczema sufferers. Later on (Chapters 8 and 9) we will also look at natural and safe methods of inhibiting excessive histamine release.

INFLAMMATION: THE NEGATIVE EFFECTS

While it is important and maybe even somewhat comforting to know that inflammation is a necessary function, unfortunately there is a 'diminishing return' to this process over time. When inflammation is chronic and does not accomplish a more immediate repair, certain chemical reactions cause the tissue destruction to worsen, and the body finds it more and more difficult to heal itself.

CHAPTER 4

Causes of Eczema

Eczema is unquestionably one of the more complex skin conditions. The fact that it appears most frequently in infants makes it quite unusual in itself, but even more bizarre is the fact that it seems to disappear in about 50 per cent of cases by the time the child is about 18 months old. Although such strange patterns may make a condition easier to diagnose and differentiate from other disorders, the fact that so many of the sufferers are not yet able to communicate properly poses significant difficulties as well. In addition, medical treatments on infants create their own set of problems. Nevertheless, the research which has been published thus far has revealed a substantial body of evidence uncovering eczema's main causes.

ALLERGIES AND ECZEMA

Without question, the consensus shows that allergies, particularly to various foods, is at least partly to blame for eczema. This fact is rather a double-edged sword. On the one hand, if the problem is being triggered by an allergic reaction, such as to a food, then avoidance of the offending food should reduce the need for medication, which might itself pose problems. On the other hand, and especially with the many non-infant sufferers, avoidance of a particular food or foods is not always going to be complied with. This is bad enough when sufferers are faced with eliminating a food (often one of their favourites) and they do not want to make the sacrifice. Even worse is the fact that, chances are, they will not even know *which* food or foods is causing the eczema in the first place.

Food allergies are a very involved subject and are known to be a factor in many different health disorders. Far too lengthy to discuss in its entirety here, we will look briefly into the topic to create a better understanding of what may cause the eczema reaction.

Which food or foods someone is allergic to depends on the individual, but research into childhood eczema seems to suggest that milk products are the most common food allergen in infants. Research also shows that not only eczema but also its related allergic condition, asthma, are often associated with a dairy allergy. Many infants who suffer with eczema will go on to develop asthma later on. This point is particularly important due to the fact that asthma can be quite a severe medical condition. Understanding the strong association with childhood eczema and properly dealing with any food allergies may well help to reduce or avoid the negative impact of such consequences later.

Another interesting fact about food allergy-related eczema is its strong hereditary association. Eczema research has suggested that between 60 and 70 per cent of all sufferers have family members who have eczema as well. More evidence still has been produced by food allergy research, which shows that when one parent is allergic, a third of his or her offspring will have allergies. If both parents are allergic, about two-thirds of their children will have allergies.

These are definitive results indeed, and go a long way to explain the need to understand and consider your own health as well as that of your child. After all, knowing such information about yourself can help you to establish a suitable diet for your baby, as well as help to keep you on the lookout for possible allergic causes underlying various unexplained symptoms. There is growing professional opinion that a substantial percentage of all undiagnosed symptoms are likely to be caused by food allergies or intolerance. In eczema, of course, this is proven to be the case.

Many different foods are known to produce allergic reactions such as eczema in susceptible (atopic) individuals. A list of some of the more common include:

- milk and other dairy products
- wheat (most breads, pasta, etc.)
- eggs
- citrus fruits
- corn (especially common in the United States)
- certain nuts.

Naturally, if it is known that food allergies are at least partly responsible for eczema, it stands to reason that avoidance of the allergy-causing food will considerably improve the condition. This is often the case, as studies have shown. Nevertheless, there are still some issues which need to be addressed. First, there is the issue of knowing *which* foods are actually causing the problem. Secondly is the need to deal with the issues which allow the person to be so allergic in the first place. Thirdly are the other factors which make it possible for eczema to occur, which must also be dealt with. In addition, it is important to correct the problems in the skin itself which allow the eczema to take hold and remain a problem. Finally, it is vital to incorporate any suitable methods of speeding the healing process whether or not the offending foods have been eliminated. All these issues will be covered within the following sections of this book.

Allergies and the Immune System

In order better to understand the substantial role food allergies play in eczema, it may be helpful to provide a brief explanation of how food allergies occur. This explanation does not go into great depth, so it is recommended that you read *Allergies* by this author (Thorsons, 1994). This book not only discusses allergies of all types in depth, but also provides a detailed look at diagnosing and treating them.

THE IMMUNE SYSTEM

The *immune system* is the body's network for protecting itself from disease by identifying, attacking and ultimately destroying harmful cancer cells, bacteria, viruses and other invaders.

The body uses *antibodies* produced by certain *white blood cells* of the immune system to identify the invaders. In doing so, the antibodies attach themselves to the invaders, 'computerize' their identity and signal other white blood cells to destroy the offending substances. This is a very neat and tidy arrangement and is absolutely necessary for life to be sustained.

Vaccinations follow this same identification and computerization technique. If, for instance, a person is being vaccinated for smallpox, the vaccine actually contains smallpox, but in an amount designed to be too tiny to present a problem. Introducing this small amount of 'invading material' triggers the person's antibodies to attach to and 'remember' the identity of smallpox from then on, so that if the person is ever exposed to larger amounts of smallpox, the immune system will quickly recognize it and destroy it before it creates a serious problem.

This is where the explanation of allergies really begins. Certain components in food are not supposed to be absorbed into the bloodstream until they are digested completely into a form that the body can use. Sometimes, incompletely digested food components (especially proteins) inadvertently get absorbed anyway. The problem is that, in this form, they can be treated as harmful invaders by antibodies, which will attach themselves, computerize the identity, and signal an attack.

The intestines are designed not to let large amounts of undigested food proteins into the bloodstream. A weakened intestinal wall could, however, allow this to occur. As a result, in order for a food allergy reaction to occur, poor digestion (particularly of protein) and a weakened intestinal tract would be the two major contributors.

This said, the question still remains as to why such an attack would be responsible for an allergic reaction such as eczema, especially when it would appear that the immune system is just doing its normal job?

This too is a long story, but a simple answer is that an immune system can attack the food allergen (antigen) in many different locations of the body. A chronic immune system attack, especially if occurring in an area where the nearby tissue is already weakened, can create further damage and irritation in the area. Ultimately, the ensuing damage and irritation stimulate the release of inflammatory chemicals such as histamine, leukotrienes and certain prostaglandins to initiate the healing process. If the weakened area happens to be the skin tissue, eczema can be the result.

Diagnosis of Food Allergies

Now that we have covered how allergies work to produce eczema, it is also vital to know how to identify the offending foods. Ultimately, rather than guessing what is responsible you must have allergies properly diagnosed. This is a controversial subject in itself, as there is currently no such thing as an allergy testing method which is 100 per cent accurate. Nevertheless, there are methods which are better than most, as well as those that have practicality as their strong point. Some are based on specialized blood testing, while others can be done at home. Although allergy diagnosis is too detailed to cover here in its entirety, for your reference we will take a brief look at a couple of the methods perhaps best suited to eczema sufferers.

ELIMINATION/REINTRODUCTION DIETS

In spite of the fact that certain blood tests may offer the most specific diagnostic capability, one of the do-it-yourself approaches has some distinct advantages. This is known as *challenge testing* and involves eliminating likely allergens for a period and then reintroducing them later to gauge any untoward reaction.

The premise of such an approach is sound, because if someone eliminates allergens in the diet for a period of time, he or she often becomes especially sensitive to the foods he or she is allergic to. Upon reintroducing them into the diet, it is often easier to analyse which foods produce an adverse reaction such as eczema.

It is important to note that this type of testing should not be used with those who suffer from food allergy-induced asthma or other potentially dangerous allergic reactions. The best available blood test (e.g. RAST testing – see below) does not require ingestion of the food, and thus does not risk a reaction. This should be used instead in such cases. Challenge testing is also problematic for infants, as proper communication is not possible and the parent cannot pacify the child should there be any challenge-induced reaction. Nevertheless, this method can be very valuable, not only because it can help identify offending foods, but also because it does not involve any expense.

The major steps to the elimination/challenge testing are as follows:

1. For one to four weeks straight, avoid all foods except for the following:
   - lamb
   - poultry
   - certain vegetables (e.g. broccoli, cauliflower, carrots, cabbage)
   - rice
   - potatoes
   - pears and apples.

   The reason for this strict list is that this generally eliminates the most common allergy-causing foods. The period of time required allows the body to rid itself of the offending food components responsible for any allergies and also serves to heighten the sensitivity of the person and thereby make more apparent any reaction when foods are reintroduced. (It is possible for a person to be allergic to one of the foods on the above list, but it is far less likely.)

2. After the one to four weeks has expired, the major foods left out of the above list are reintroduced, ONE AT A TIME. It must be done this way, otherwise the sufferer would not know exactly which food was causing a reaction. Each food should be reintroduced for a

couple of days in a row before adding another to the diet.

Many allergic reactions, especially in the case of eczema flare-ups, are delayed reactions, so you may need a couple of days to see a reaction. If you experience a reaction in less than a couple of days, make a record of the reaction and the food responsible and stop eating the food. Even if the reaction occurs early on and the offending food is eliminated from the diet, you should still wait a few days before adding the next food. This allows the previous reaction to run its course and leave the body.

3. Once you have reintroduced all of the foods that you intended testing, keep a record of the results, including the offending food, the time it took for a reaction to occur, how the reaction manifested itself (e.g. eczema, bloating, headache, etc.), and how severe the reaction was.

Once the offending foods have been discovered, the natural assumption is that the food will have to be avoided forever. Fortunately, this is seldom the case.

There are two types of food allergies: *cyclic* and *fixed*. In a cyclic allergy, which the vast majority of allergies are, sufferers will experience an allergic reaction if they consume the food allergen in large quantities and/or very frequently. It seems that only when they pass a certain threshold, the reaction occurs; by eliminating the food for a period of time they can eventually tolerate it again – provided they consume it only in small quantities, and only occasionally.

There is a special method for accomplishing this, called a *rotation diet*. This allows those foods responsible for cyclic allergies to be consumed in small quantities approximately once a week. This may well avoid passing the 'allergy threshold'. Sufferers will know if they have overdone it, or if theirs is not a cyclic allergy, if they have a reaction while attempting the rotation diet.

In the case of a fixed allergy, the person will react adversely even with the period of avoidance and generally even if small quantities are consumed infrequently. These foods should be avoided completely and indefinitely, although very occasionally a sufferer might re-establish tolerance for a fixed allergy food after a very long period of avoidance. Rotation diets should not include any food which is known to cause a potentially dangerous allergic reaction, just in case you inadvertently pass the tolerance threshold. Such diets, while often very useful, are not perfect or scientifically exact and may require adjustment on occasion. Keeping a good record until a workable routine is established is very important.

In addition to the inconvenience of going through the entire process, challenge testing can only determine general food reactions. Not all adverse reactions to foods are caused by an allergy to the food itself. Nevertheless, challenge testing can at least give you a good picture of what foods should be avoided and rotated.

RAST TEST

One of the most accurate diagnostic procedures involves a blood analysis called a *RAST test* (radio allergo sorbent test). This test involves measuring the binding of blood antibodies to the food substance being tested.

As this test is not performed within the body it is well suited for those circumstances when challenge testing is inappropriate or too inconvenient. In addition, RAST testing can diagnose allergies specifically and will not confuse them with non-allergic reactions.

The two disadvantages of RAST tests are a) it can be relatively expensive when testing for several different foods, and b) RAST testing looks for more immediate allergies and is not as accurate for allergies which take some time to manifest. As a result, it is often recommended that you eat the food being tested two or three days' prior to being tested for it. This allows the allergic process to take better hold by the time of the test. This pre-test consumption should NOT, of course, be done by anyone who experiences severe or potentially dangerous allergic reactions to the tested foods.

No matter what method is used, allergy diagnosis is a very crucial step in a complete eczema therapy programme. Although in later chapters effective natural treatments for inflammatory skin reactions will be discussed, they should preferably not be used in place of any necessary dietary changes. In addition, even if eczema is the obvious manifestation of your allergy, if allowed to thrive unchecked allergies can be harmful to the body in general.

WEAKNESS OF SKIN

Although allergies may be responsible for much of the origin of eczema, there are other factors which can account for the fact that the allergic reaction appears on the skin rather than elsewhere. In addition, there can be characteristics of the skin of eczema sufferers which can prevent the lesions from healing or induce their spread.

Aside from the itchy, dry and thickened characteristics of eczemic skin, one of the main dysfunctions found in the skin of eczema sufferers relates to the local response of the immune system.

We just looked into the adverse effect of an immune system activated toward food allergens. As it turns out, research shows that at the same time there is actually a reduced ability of local 'attacking' white blood cells to kill bacteria in the affected skin.

This abnormality is significant because eczemic skin is almost always severely infected by the bacteria *staphylococcus aureus*. The white blood cells responsible for destroying such bacteria appear less capable of doing so, thus allowing this harmful organism to take hold.

There are other types of harmful organisms which are more prominent in such cases as well. This bacterial overgrowth not only weakens the skin in general, but prevents proper healing of the skin and can easily spread to other eczemic areas. Scientific analysis of eczema sufferers shows that this immune dysfunction fluctuates in direct correlation with the improvement and worsening of the eczema. For all these reasons, it is clear that controlling the growth of this bacteria would be a major priority in the treatment of eczema; a natural approach to tackling this will be discussed in Chapter 8.

NUTRITIONAL DEFICIENCIES AND ECZEMA

There is clear evidence that dietary mismanagement can have a devastating effect on the health of the skin in general. Eczemic skin is definitely no exception. Not only eating too much of the wrong thing, but also getting too few of the nutrients that strengthen the skin, promote healing and proper immune function, reduce inflammation, etc. are factors in eczema. Chapters 7, 8 and 9 are devoted to this subject; it is highly recommended that you study them thoroughly. They contain information

on the dietary, nutritional and also herbal factors which
have been medically and scientifically proven to be effective in eczema therapy and/or its cause – without the
high risk of damaging side-effects or toxicity.

STRESS AND ECZEMA

It should not come as a big surprise to discover that stress
can cause a worsening of eczema. Stress literally affects the
functioning of the body in so many negative ways that it
would be very difficult to trace the exact reason why it
aggravates this condition. It can only be covered here
very briefly, but suffice it to say that stress reduction,
whether through relaxation techniques, nutritional means
or any other method, would be of great value to any
eczema sufferer.

Stress may aggravate eczema in several ways, such as by:

- causing a depletion of certain nutrients (e.g. vitamins
  and minerals) which are essential for the proper health
  of the skin and the control of eczema

- weakening the function of the *adrenal glands*
  The adrenal glands are responsible for hormonal
  suppression of inflammation and allergic reactions,
  as well as for controlling stress reactions. They can
  produce and release a class of hormones called *corticosteroids* and the hormone *adrenaline* to carry out this
  purpose. Interestingly, corticosteroid cremes containing *hydrocortisone* are often prescribed by dermatologists
  for eczema. In spite of temporarily reducing the
  eczemic inflammation, if used frequently these cremes
  can damage the skin. The natural hormonal release
  from the adrenals does not carry such risks, and any-

thing which maintains the strength of the adrenal glands will benefit eczema sufferers.

- causing immune system dysfunction
  Stress, especially if chronic and/or severe, can adversely affect the functioning of the immune system. This dysfunction can be manifested in many ways and would be most unhelpful in the case of eczema.

Once you understand the factors that can cause and/or exacerbate eczema it is much easier to choose a course of action. Correcting the causes of eczema not only helps you to gain control over the disorder itself, but also invariably has either an eventual or immediate positive effect on the symptoms.

CHAPTER 5

Causes of Psoriasis

In Chapter 2 we looked at how psoriasis manifests on the skin, as well as the fact that there are other tissues of the body that are often affected. This in itself points out the fact that addressing only the more obvious skin manifestation will not correct the condition in its entirety. Even if someone with psoriasis has problems only with his or her skin, this would still be the case. It is clear from the research that what damages the health and function of the skin does not originate in skin tissue itself.

As you know, the most obvious symptom of psoriasis is the excessive shedding of skin cells, which shows up as silvery scales atop reddened patches. These scales of skin are allowed to develop by what seems to be a very simple and logical explanation: The skin cells are dividing too fast for the body to be able to shed them as it normally would.

The tissues of your body (such as those of the skin) are made up of countless cells, each of which has its own life-sustaining mechanisms within it. A part of these inner workings allows the cells to divide in order to produce other cells of the same type so that there is a constant replacement of worn-out cells with fresh, new and healthy ones. This is how tissues in the body continue to function for so many decades. In this same way, dead skin cells are replaced by new ones, which will eventually die while others are produced to replace them, and so on. Each cell within the body will divide at a rate that is determined by a mechanism within the cell itself.

CYCLIC AMP AND GMP

The mechanism which controls the rate at which this division of cells occurs is regulated by two cellular substances known as *cyclic adenosine monophosphate (cAMP)* and *cyclic guanosine monophosphate (cGMP)*. These substances are used by the body as messengers which help trigger certain cellular activities. Ultimately, the range of their effects can be quite vast, but where skin cell replication is concerned there are two main points of significance.

Cyclic AMP is needed to catalyse certain chemical processes within the cells which allow it to continue to function and mature. The longer the skin cells can continue to reach their full potential for maturation, as a result of higher levels of cAMP, the longer this cell multiplication is delayed. The messenger cGMP, on the other hand, seems to trigger an accelerated rate of cell multiplication.

Considering these discoveries, it is not surprising that analysis of the skin cells of psoriasis sufferers has revealed an excessive cGMP activity in comparison to cAMP. Clearly such an imbalance not only encourages the main symptom pattern we see in psoriasis, but is inappropriate for the proper health of these cells in general. The resultant mess leads to a piling up of skin cells at a rate which the body cannot cope with.

What causes this imbalance in the first place? The reasons can vary somewhat, but it is known that various damaging agents may alter the proportion between the two messengers. These damaging agents include intestinal toxins and free radicals.

INTESTINAL TOXINS

There are several toxins which are quite capable of creating havoc in the body. Alteration of the cAMP:cGMP ratio is just one example of this. The problem is, many such toxins are produced from within the body and are not very easy either to prevent or eliminate.

Perhaps the most troublesome toxins in the case of psoriasis are ones that are prominent in the intestinal tract. If such toxins are absorbed through the intestinal wall into the bloodstream, the implications for the body's cells can be disastrous. Some of the most damaging include:

- components from certain types of bacteria (e.g. certain streptococcal strains)
- the yeast/fungus *candida albicans*
- byproducts of allergic reactions, especially to foods
- byproducts of bacterial protein breakdown

Bacteria

Clearly, harmful bacteria have a great deal to answer for in the case of psoriasis. In some cases, the cell walls from such bacteria can be absorbed and interfere with proper cell chemistry. Although we are constantly exposed to harmful bacteria in the intestinal tract, there are other types of beneficial bacteria which are intended to help keep the harmful types under control. Unfortunately, this does not always work as it is supposed to.

Aside from parts of the bacteria itself causing the problem, certain functions of these harmful organisms must be stopped as well. One of the most destructive effects of bacteria relates to what it can do to protein within the body.

Protein from the foods we eat is supposed to be broken down into *amino acids* during the digestive process within the stomach and the first part of the intestinal tract. This process is intended to be accomplished by various *digestive enzymes*. Eventually, the amino acids are to be absorbed into the bloodstream from the intestines in order to nourish the body.

If this process does not occur as intended, certain bacteria may act upon the amino acids, producing in the process harmful toxins called *polyamines*. One of the most destructive effects of polyamines is an imbalancing of cAMP and cGMP, in this case to the favour of accelerated cell proliferation.

If the digestive processes are working properly this should not occur to any great extent; strengthening the digestive system should be a main priority in any psoriasis programme (see Chapter 9).

Candida Albicans

Another harmful organism is a type of yeast called *candida albicans*. This is a common resident of the human intestine, but occasionally it can spread out of control due to certain circumstances such as treatment with certain medication (e.g. antibiotics, corticosteroids, birth control pills, antacids); digestive enzyme deficiencies; dietary mismanagement (e.g. excessive sugar and alcohol intake); immune system weakness, etc.

Toxins produced from the yeast (which can eventually turn into a more damaging fungal form) can produce problems and, at a given point, candida albicans itself can infiltrate the bloodstream, thus producing some of its most significant damage. Such damage can include adverse effects on cAMP:cGMP ratios.

Food Allergies

At this point, it is advised that you refer to Chapter 4 (Allergies and Eczema) for a more complete discussion of food allergies. If you have already read this chapter, you may recall that when someone is allergic to a particular food substance, certain antibodies from the immune system will bind to the substance in order to initiate its destruction. The resulting damage is substantial in the case of eczema, but would also be quite unhelpful in psoriasis. The complexes produced when the antibody binds with the food substance and causes the allergy can themselves alter cell function in the same way that harmful bacteria and *candida* can.

OTHER DAMAGING FACTORS

Psoriasis can be affected adversely by exposure to countless negative influences. This, of course, makes it one of the more difficult conditions to control, especially if sufferers attempt to accomplish this merely by trying to avoid these negative influences.

Free Radicals

Free radicals are molecules or chemical fragments that are very reactive and potentially very damaging. They can be derived from or produced by exposure to many different sources. Some of the more common sources include environmental pollution, tobacco smoke, radiation, cooked fats and alcohol; many free radicals are even produced during normal and necessary processes within our bodies. A complete discussion of free radicals and the damage they produce would require an in-depth chemistry lecture, but suffice it to say that various free radicals can be particularly damaging both to skin tissue and to the cAMP:cGMP ratio. In addition, they can indirectly cause inflammation.

As a large percentage of the free radicals we are exposed to originate from our own bodies during essential chemical reactions, such as during energy utilization, they cannot be completely avoided. Anyone can, however, realistically reduce the outside exposure to at least a small extent, and can significantly reduce the damage caused by free radicals, no matter their source, by certain measures which will be discussed in Chapter 9.

Stress

Stress, in so many forms, is an unavoidable fact of life which can exacerbate so many different health disorders. Many sufferers of both eczema and psoriasis find that stress can trigger an outbreak.

There are many reasons why this stress-induced exacerbation may occur in psoriasis, such as: weakening of the digestive system (e.g. reducing digestive enzyme levels); the depletion of certain vitamins and minerals which are needed for proper health of the skin tissue; weakening the adrenal glands which help control reactions during inflammatory skin disorders; and others.

The extent of the connection between stress and psoriasis has been researched by the medical and scientific community. One such study published in the *British Journal of Dermatology* showed that almost one in four psoriasis patients suffers particular acute stress shortly before the first manifestation of the condition. Relaxation techniques have offered significant benefits to many sufferers.

PSORIASIS AND LIVER FUNCTION

All you need do is read the above paragraphs to see just some of the vast array of toxic substances that can cause damage to the body and that can cause or exacerbate psoriasis.

Nevertheless, the body is capable of neutralizing the effect of such harmful influences and thus preventing associated health problems. If the agent or toxin succeeds in entering the bloodstream, whether through the intestines or elsewhere, the body has a process whereby the blood is filtered of harmful substances BEFORE they can do serious damage to the tissue cells. This filtering device is the liver.

Actually, the liver plays so many necessary roles in human biochemistry that improving its function is doubtlessly an important measure in the fight against any health disorder. As one of its major functions relates to detoxifying harmful substances in the bloodstream, the liver is especially vital to the prevention and treatment of psoriasis.

As a result, it is obvious that one of the most important goals of any psoriasis sufferer should be to improve liver function (see Chapter 9). Nevertheless, it is important to note here that the efficiency of liver function is relative. Someone who is exposed to a minimum of toxins will not need as strong a liver as someone who is exposed to many. For this reason, in addition to bolstering the liver (e.g. by methods to be discussed later on), it is best to avoid anything that is likely to over-tax the liver, especially those substances that also disrupt the cAMP:cGMP ratio.

GENERAL SKIN HEALTH

In both psoriasis and eczema, the general health of the skin will have a bearing on the manifestation of the condition. As a matter of fact, the health of the skin, or lack thereof, can be critical as to whether the skin will even be affected in the first place.

If we look at the causes of psoriasis we find that there are many other health disorders associated with the same causes, where the skin is not the prime site of infection.

For example, intestinal toxicity, polyamine production and food allergy byproducts are also common factors in certain forms of arthritis. Not all the people whose arthritis is either caused or made worse by these factors will develop psoriasis; nevertheless, the strong link between psoriasis and arthritis is most likely due to the similarity of the potential causes. If there is weakness in the skin tissue and the joints to begin with, this increases the likelihood of developing both conditions (either simultaneously or at different points in one's life). This connection is somewhat similar to the relationship between eczema and asthma. As a result, any efforts to strengthen the skin tissue can help avert the course of such related disorders.

PART III

Dietary Control

CHAPTER 6

Eczema, Psoriasis and Improper Diet

As you can probably imagine, the dietary recommendations for combating eczema or psoriasis can be complex. While there are some very important general considerations for all eczema or psoriasis sufferers, the fact that food allergies can play a primary role must also be considered.

Although food allergies may play a more pivotal role in eczema, as mentioned before, complexes comprised of antibodies and allergy-causing food components can adversely alter cAMP:cGMP ratios in psoriasis. The role of food allergies in these conditions makes matters especially confusing, because many of the foods which commonly cause allergic reactions are highly nutritious and 'healthy'.

ALLERGY DIAGNOSIS

A first priority for any sufferer should perhaps be to begin the process of identifying which foods may be causing an allergic reaction (please review Chapter 4 – Allergies and Eczema). If the method used is a blood test (e.g. RAST testing), this may help take some of the guesswork out of the process.

Many people, for various reasons, will choose to use the elimination/challenge testing diets, and these can indeed be very useful in assessing which foods might be the culprits. Remember that once you find a food which produces a reaction, it may well not be the only one, so you should complete the testing procedure as directed in Chapter 4. Once identification has been made, then you may eventually be able to tolerate small amounts of the food on a rotation basis, but this should only be done within the parameters set by the rotation diet, and only if no reaction occurs.

You should not bypass the step of identifying or diagnosing any possible food allergy. If you don't follow a specific procedure, at least consider trying to avoid for a period of time some of the most common offenders (such as dairy products – milk, cheese, etc. – and wheat products – most breads, pasta, etc.) to see if it helps your condition.

ANIMAL FATS

As mentioned in Chapters 3 and 4, inflammation can definitely be affected by one's diet. Food allergy reactions cause the release of large amounts of inflammatory histamine, and a fatty acid called arachidonic acid causes inflammatory reactions due to the production of leukotrienes and prostaglandin E2 (PGE2).

Clearly, avoiding foods you are allergic to will significantly reduce histamine levels in affected tissues, and avoiding arachidonic acid can be of great value in inhibiting inflammation as well. As arachidonic acid is found in animal foods (e.g. meat, dairy products, etc.), one of your first dietary goals should be to reduce or possibly eliminate the intake of animal fats. If you still want to consume some form of meat, a better choice would be the white meat of poultry, as this generally has a lower total fat level.

The extent to which this regime would have to be followed depends on the severity of the inflammation. The excessive intake of animal fats also reduces the activity of certain other types of fat substances which are actually beneficial to the general health and function of the skin tissue.

Fats and Free Radicals

These days it is common for many people to think of animal fats as being 'unhealthy', while vegetable fats are considered 'healthy'. Although from a general dietary standpoint, vegetable oils are better than large quantities of animal fats, there are times when vegetable oils can present a significant problem to health as well.

From a strictly nutritional angle, vegetable oils, by providing high levels of *unsaturated fat*, can give the body what it needs to make certain essential fatty acids (EFAs) which are needed to sustain life. These fatty acids can be used for this purpose efficiently – provided the oils are *uncooked*. The higher the temperature to which unsaturated fats (especially polyunsaturated types) are exposed, the more their chemical structure is altered; ultimately this can make them unable to carry out certain beneficial functions. In addition, heated vegetable oils produce high levels of certain free radicals (mentioned in Chapter 4) which can damage the integrity of the skin and encourage inflammation.

For these reasons, cooked vegetable oils (especially those used in frying) should be significantly reduced. In order to get the benefits that vegetable oils can provide, use them in their raw state, such as in salad dressings.

STIMULANTS

When most people hear the word 'stimulants' they probably think of drugs or something of the sort. Well, in this case the 'drugs' are ones that are frequently derived from our daily food and beverage intake. It is important to look at some of these 'dietary stimulants' and how they can present such a problem to eczema or psoriasis sufferers.

Sugar

One of the first types of stimulant you should try to limit in your diet is sugar. The reasons for this are far too diverse to cover completely here, and it may seem a bit trite to criticize having too much sugar in your diet, but it must be understood that there are some very specific ways that sugar can adversely affect these two skin disorders.

The first thing to be aware of is the effect of sugar on the adrenal glands. As mentioned in Chapter 4, the adrenal glands release certain hormones such as adrenaline and corticosteroids. These are responsible for initiating and controlling stress reactions, and can also suppress inflammation.

Sugar triggers an indiscriminant release of adrenaline. If the sugar intake is substantial, the released adrenaline can prompt symptoms of the first stages of acute stress. Stress reactions are sometimes necessary (as when faced by actual danger or any other stressor), but the indiscriminate release of stress hormones is very undesirable indeed. Thus sugar gives you the symptoms of a stress reaction, without serving any helpful purpose. This accounts for at least some of the nervousness or jitteriness some people experience after eating a lot of sugary foods.

Another problem is that while sugar causes the release of adrenaline, it does not replenish the supply in the adrenal gland. If you consume excessive sugar regularly, this could lower the availability of adrenaline and thus weaken the adrenal glands' ability to initiate necessary stress reactions or suppress inflammation.

Stress hormones can have adverse effects themselves, especially when serving no specific beneficial purpose at the time. Among other things, they are known to inhibit the activity of digestive enzymes (thereby increasing the risk of food allergies and polyamine production). Of course, it is already known that stress itself may trigger reactions in both disorders, so anything that disturbs the intended purpose of the adrenal glands and their hormones is to be avoided.

The excessive intake of sugar is also known to deplete levels of certain vitamins and minerals that are especially important to the health of the skin, the proper functioning of the digestive system, the immune system, stress tolerance, and countless other purposes. Needless to say, the reduction caused by sugar in the levels of these important nutrients is undesirable.

None of these concerns necessarily means that an eczema or psoriasis sufferer has to avoid completely even small amounts of sugar taken on a very occasional basis, but the less sugar you eat, the better.

Caffeine

Unfortunately, caffeine can cause many of the same problems that sugar causes for eczema and psoriasis sufferers. Caffeine also triggers the indiscriminant release of adrenaline, thus excess amounts may weaken the adrenals and waste their hormonal supply. Caffeine is also known to deplete or inhibit the absorption of certain important nutrients.

The most common sources of caffeine include:
- coffee
- tea

- chocolate
- caffeinated soft drinks (e.g. colas).

Caffeine, like sugar, may be acceptable for many eczema or psoriasis sufferers in small amounts, taken occasionally; however, as some of the potentially harmful effects of sugar and caffeine overlap, if they are both being consumed, the amounts of each should be reduced even further. Ultimately, the most prudent approach would be elimination. After all, caffeine is not required by the body whatsoever; and the essential requirements that sugar fulfils can be provided, WITHOUT the problems, from *complex carbohydrates* such as whole grains (brown rice, whole wheat, oats, etc.), pasta, potatoes, wholemeal bread and legumes. (Remember that wheat is a highly allergenic food, and may need to be avoided if you discover you are allergic to it.)

Tobacco
Although it is not a food, it is important to mention tobacco at this time, as *nicotine* is yet another stimulant which produces negative effects on the adrenal glands as well as causing a significant depletion of various important nutrients.

We are all familiar with at least some of the risks of smoking. Many of the better-known risks are related to the damage caused by smoke to the cells of the lungs.

As it turns out, the primary agents that damage the lungs are free radicals. As mentioned in Chapter 4, many free radicals are capable of damaging the skin cells and of triggering certain inflammatory processes.

Alcohol
Alcohol is not classed as a stimulant itself, but believe it or

not it too causes a release of adrenaline and depletes several nutrients that are critical not only to the skin but also to body systems which, when dysfunctional, can adversely affect both eczema and psoriasis. As we will look at now, this is particularly the case with psoriasis.

ALCOHOL AND PSORIASIS

As with tobacco, some of the problems of drinking too much are well known to many, such as the fact that alcohol can harm the liver. Usually, we associate the effect of alcohol on the liver with alcoholics, or at least those who drink larger amounts, but there are times when even smaller amounts of alcohol can lead to trouble.

If we recap the list of common causes of psoriasis, we are talking about various factors such as:

- components from certain types of bacteria (e.g. certain streptococcal strains)
- candida albicans
- antibody/allergen complexes
- polyamines (from protein breakdown by bacteria)
- free radicals.

This entire list is made up of substances that can do untold damage to the body in many more ways than just by contributing to psoriasis. Once such an agent manages to circulate freely through the system and afflict the cells, the more destructive processes begin to occur.

As mentioned in Chapter 5, under optimal circumstances the liver is capable of neutralizing such agents, or at least neutralizing the byproducts of the reactions produced by the agents. Unfortunately, it would appear that the liver in a typical psoriasis sufferer is often incapable of detoxifying in an efficient manner.

As you might have guessed, if liver functioning has been impaired, as is often the case with alcohol consumption, then this filtering process is less effective and thus many harmful agents may be allowed to roam free and cause cellular damage, such as is seen in psoriasis.

There is yet another concern with alcohol which makes the reduced ability of the liver to detoxify even more worrying. It seems that the consumption of alcohol also allows a greater quantity of intestinally-derived toxins to be absorbed into the bloodstream in the first place. This, of course, is the last thing anyone with psoriasis needs.

The medical research states that alcohol is definitely a particular problem in psoriasis. All of the above toxins can alter cAMP and cGMP ratios; for a healthy liver, detoxifying them is no problem. But alcohol increases the likelihood of larger amounts of toxins being absorbed into the bloodstream; for this reason alcohol should be avoided by psoriasis sufferers. This is one of the cases where complete abstention is urged, as the liver of a psoriasis sufferer can ill afford the stress that alcohol (even in moderation) brings. Needless to say, however, if you still decide to consume alcohol, then the less you drink, the better. (It should be stressed that alcohol consumption, especially in excess, also causes problems for eczema sufferers in that it adversely affects the liver's ability to filter allergens, etc.)

CHAPTER 7

Eating to Combat Eczema and Psoriasis

Although the dietary restrictions for both eczema and psoriasis are rather lengthy, there are certain foods you should strongly consider eating in larger quantities. It just so happens that those who eat too many of the wrong foods are perhaps much more likely also to eat too little of the right ones, so shifting the emphasis can make a world of difference. Especially in the case of eczema, dietary changes can often yield noticeable benefits on their own; for many sufferers these benefits can come about quite early in the programme. At worst, such changes should at least keep matters from getting much worse.

> **PLEASE NOTE:** When considering the following list of beneficial dietary steps it is important to note that any beneficial food which you happen to be allergic to should not be consumed, even if it may generally benefit most sufferers. If in any doubt, please consult a qualified health practitioner.

BENEFICIAL FATS

In spite of the disastrous effects of certain types of fats discussed in Chapter 6, conversely there are some types of fats that can be quite beneficial and even therapeutic in the fight against eczema and psoriasis. Although these will be discussed in more detail in Chapters 8 and 9, they are worth a brief mention here.

Typically, people consider the only notable difference between fats to be whether they are saturated or unsaturated, or perhaps whether they are animal or vegetable fats. These are indeed important distinctions, especially to general health, but there are other issues that may be even more important to the subject of eczema and psoriasis. The following are some of the most common fat-containing foods:

- meats (e.g. beef, pork, lamb, etc.)
- dairy products (e.g. milk, cheese, etc.)
- poultry
- fish
- eggs
- vegetable oils
- nuts and seeds
- whole grains
- beans (e.g. soya beans).

The type of fat depends on the type of food, but animal products typically contain higher amounts of saturated fats. Vegetable oils, fatty fish (e.g. salmon, mackerel and herring), nuts and seeds, whole grains and beans are particularly rich in unsaturated fats (especially the poly-unsaturated variety).

The body breaks down fats into fatty acids. Your body requires certain fatty acids (called *essential fatty acids* or *EFAs*) to manufacture substances that are vital to life. Without an adequate supply of the EFAs (*linoleic acid* and *linolenic acid*), our bodies could not function.

Your dietary goal should be to consume foods containing unsaturated fats (thus the EFAs) and moderate your intake of saturated fats. However, as you may recall from Chapter 6 it is important to make sure that the unsaturated fats are not cooked first – for example, if vegetable oils are used as sources of EFAs, they should mostly be consumed in their raw state, such as in salads.

A generous intake of unsaturated EFAs may also help to offset some of the inflammatory problems associated with the high levels of arachidonic acid found in animal fats. This will be discussed in more detail in Chapters 8 and 9.

Oily Fish

The fats found in high concentrations in certain types of fatty fish (such as salmon, mackerel and herring) are known as *omega 3 fatty acids*. These fatty acids have a particularly powerful anti-inflammatory effect (see Chapter 8). To derive the full benefits, it is best to cook them by poaching or steaming. Alternatively, very concentrated amounts of omega 3 fatty acids can be obtained through fish oil supplements (see Chapter 9). (This is only to be recommended, of course, if you are not allergic to such fish.)

ANTIOXIDANT-RICH FOODS

As discussed earlier, harmful agents known as free radicals can play a destructive role in the development of inflammatory skin disorders. Aside from the filtering role of the liver, nature has a way of combating and neutralizing the effect of free radicals before they have the opportunity to do their damage. This neutralization is carried out by substances known as *antioxidants* (see Chapters 8 and 9). Some of the most important antioxidants include the following nutrients:

- beta carotene (plant pigment)
- vitamin A
- vitamin C
- vitamin E
- selenium (a trace mineral)
- l-cysteine (an amino acid)
- zinc (a trace mineral).

Some of the richest dietary sources of these nutrients are:

- fresh vegetables
- fresh fruit
- whole grains (brown rice, wheat, oats, etc.)
- beans
- raw seeds and nuts.

Following an eating plan that consists of larger amounts of foods from the above list (except those you are allergic to) would be beneficial to any eczema or psoriasis sufferer.

Many antioxidant nutrients also play a helpful part in strengthening and healing the skin tissue in general.

DIETARY FIBRE

There is another bonus to eating high-antioxidant foods such as fruits, vegetables, whole grains, nuts, seeds, beans and so on. These are also the best sources of *dietary fibre*.

Many people are familiar with the countless recommendations to increase fibre intake in the diet, yet statistics tell us that the vast majority do not consume enough for optimal health. The better-known connection between fibre and health has normally focused on the treatment of constipation, reducing the risk of colon diseases and certain weight control requirements. It can also be of great value in eczema and psoriasis.

What Is Fibre?

Fibre is the primarily indigestible portion of non-animal foods. There are several different types of fibre; the two most important classifications are *insoluble fibre* and *soluble fibre*.

Insoluble fibre, such as *cellulose*, is found in many foods such as wheat (bran) and fruits and vegetables. Insoluble fibre does not absorb moisture and thus maintains much of its original texture and integrity after ingestion, throughout the intestinal tract.

Soluble fibre is found in various fruits (including apples) and in vegetables, but also in rich quantities in various beans, seeds (e.g. psyllium) and certain whole grains such as oats (bran). Unlike insoluble fibre, the soluble form does absorb moisture and, in the process, softens and swells.

The primary function of dietary fibre is to speed the transit time of food through the digestive tract. This means that food will be eliminated much faster and more efficiently. This is important to the specific requirements of eczema and psoriasis sufferers for a few reasons:

1. If foods remain in the intestines too long, certain toxins can be produced. One example of these toxins is the family of polyamines which, as you know, are strongly linked with negatively altering the ratio of cAMP and cGMP in people with psoriasis. There are many other toxins that can exacerbate both eczema and psoriasis which would be reduced if foods were eliminated faster.
2. Because of the specific cleansing capability of dietary fibre, it can directly aid in the removal of damaging agents and organisms that have already developed in

the intestinal tract. Among others, these can include:
　harmful bacteria (including those that form
　polyamines from amino acids)
　endotoxins (from bacterial cell walls)
　byproducts of food allergens
　candida albicans.

Elimination of these damaging agents is clearly an advantage in psoriasis, but is also helpful to those with eczema.

The ability to remove so many potentially harmful intestinal toxins is especially true of soluble fibre. Because of its ability to absorb water, it can also absorb moisture-borne toxins in the gut. In addition, if the intestinal wall is weakened or sensitive, as is often the case in sufferers of these conditions, soluble fibre will be more soothing due to its softness. Certain forms of insoluble fibre, especially wheat bran, can be irritating to a weakened intestinal wall. Of course, wheat is also one of the most common food allergens in the first place.

The key in any diet for eczema or psoriasis is to achieve an allergy-free selection that contains:

- the more beneficial types of fats (e.g. raw vegetable oils)
- a rich supply of all the essential vitamins and minerals
- a generous amount of antioxidant nutrients
- high-fibre content (especially soluble fibre)
- plenty of pure water(to aid in detoxification)

Any changes will be better than none, but the more severe your condition, the more strict and diligent you should be about your dietary regime. Remember, even if you are allergic to certain foods you may eventually be able to rotate them on an occasional basis, so you are seldom going to have to eliminate anything for good. As the condition is kept under control for a period of time, such as with the aid of the supplements discussed in Chapters 8 and 9, you may be able to cut back on some if not all of these dietary restrictions. It is never to be advised, however, to eat large quantities of any food that is detrimental to your condition, even after it seems to have disappeared. People with eczema or psoriasis have a tendency that may make the condition return if they overdo it. Only trial and error will guide you in tailoring a programme that works for you over the long term, but the results can be very rewarding, to say the least!

PART IV

Therapeutic Treatment

Clearly, the only guaranteed 'cure' to any disease or disorder is to prevent it in the first place, but significant improvement can definitely be achieved with a programme that addresses the causes (and if necessary the symptoms) directly. As a matter of fact, discovering and then dealing with the underlying causes can, in many cases, more or less eliminate the symptoms. Chapters 8 and 9 are dedicated to discussing the treatment of the symptoms and causes of eczema and psoriasis.

With this is mind, it is clear from the previous chapter that a person's eating habits can play a monumental role in the course of eczema and psoriasis. Much of this is based on evidence from medical and scientific research.

There are certain limitations to the effectiveness of dietary changes, especially if your condition has deep-rooted genetic links or is particularly acute. However, the results of scientific investigation seem to suggest that certain nutritional and herbal remedies may well prove successful, especially in conjunction with dietary changes. These remedies include:

- vitamins
- minerals
- fatty acids
- digestive enzymes

- certain amino acids
- fibre
- and various herbs.

Such research, published in both medical and scientific journals, shows just how potent – and safe – items from the list above can be with respect to the correction of both the symptoms and even many of the causes of eczema and psoriasis.

It is important to note that in spite of the fact that positive results have been reported even when the supplements alone are used (without any specific dietary changes being implemented), for the best outcome you should not use the supplements instead of, but only along with, dietary changes.

DRUG TREATMENT

Treatment of both eczema and psoriasis can be a very confusing affair, although you would never know this by the standard orthodox medical treatment for these conditions. This kind of treatment, especially in the case of eczema, often involves suppressing the inflammatory skin reaction rather than attempting to correct its causes.

Clearly it is the symptoms that are paramount in the mind of the sufferer, but it should be understood that symptomatic treatment which does not alter the cause(s) will never eliminate the condition. Worse still, in the case of the most common medical treatment of these conditions, problems arise such as the reduced effectiveness of the treatment over time, and a high risk of certain side-effects. Let us look briefly at perhaps the best example of this dilemma where eczema and psoriasis are concerned.

Corticosteroids and Inflammatory Skin Disorders

In the orthodox medical treatment of eczema and psoriasis, the class of drugs called steroidal anti-inflammatory drugs (*e.g. corticosteroids)* are often used in the form of *hydrocortisone creme*.

When found as part of a hydrocortisone creme, corticosteroids are generally used in order to suppress an inflammatory skin reaction. Under some circumstances corticosteroids are used in other forms to treat disorders such as some cases of rheumatoid arthritis, multiple sclerosis (MS), systemic lupus erythematosus, severe allergic reactions (e.g. asthma), and ulcerative/inflammatory bowel disorders (e.g. Crohn's disease).

We produce corticosteroids (sometimes called 'steroids') in our adrenal glands. Among other things, these hormones suppress inflammation, control allergic reactions, help regulate long-term stress responses, suppress immune response, and carry out many different metabolic functions.

Corticosteroid drugs have the basic properties of the related hormones produced naturally in our bodies. The one major attribute of naturally produced corticosteroids, which cannot be matched by the drugs, is their regulating mechanisms. The levels and release of corticosteroids made by our bodies are controlled by the body's requirements and circumstances. When they are administered to the body from outside, these levels are not being controlled with respect to the body's moment-to-moment requirements. This is a significant issue, as corticosteroids in excessive amounts can have quite severe effects on the body. This fact is confirmed by the many well known side-effects and high toxicity of such drugs.

In the case of eczema or psoriasis, however, the method of administration is topical and local, thus many of the side-effects which normally harm the body when steroids are taken internally will not be so much of a concern. Topical cortisone can be absorbed to an extent into the system, but is far less likely to produce 'systemic' (throughout the body) effects.

In spite of this higher level of safety, the local effect of hydrocortisone is certainly not without major problems. By far the most well-known side-effect of local, topical steroids is the fact that it causes the skin to become thin. Over long-term, frequent use, this can reach a quite significant point, to where such damage becomes more or less permanent.

Symptomatically, steroids are often effective, at least in the early stages before the skin is severely damaged. It must be understood, however, that hydrocortisone, and in fact steroids in any medical form, does NOT correct or reverse or cure the condition it is treating. As it does not address the actual cause, it cannot possibly accomplish a cure. In the case of hydrocortisone cremes, you should think long and hard about measuring the benefits against the potential risks.

> **IMPORTANT:** In spite of the concerns associated with corticosteroids, you should not discontinue their use without first consulting a physician. The implications of withholding the medication, especially if immediate, can lead to a worsening of the symptoms.

Fortunately, there are many natural agents which do not carry a high risk of side-effects or toxicity, but which do possess significant anti-inflammatory effects. In addition, it just so happens that many of them, rather than damaging the skin tissue in the process, actually are known to *strengthen* the skin. These agents will be discussed in

Chapters 8 and 9.

There are also safe and natural methods that can effectively address the causes of both conditions, which not only benefit the course of the condition but also ultimately help to deal with the symptoms.

> **PLEASE NOTE:** The following information is NOT intended to be prescriptive. The author and the publisher accept no responsibility for any circumstances occurring as the result of the reader experimenting with the following programmes. Please consult a doctor before beginning this or any other new health regime.

CHAPTER 8

Nutritional and Herbal Therapy for Eczema

Considering the many factors that are involved in the development of conditions such as eczema, the body of evidence that shows that there are natural substances which address them is quite impressive.

GAMMA LINOLENIC ACID (GLA)

On the basis of published clinical research, one of the more promising nutrients in the control of eczema and its symptoms comes from the family of essential fatty acids (EFAs) mentioned earlier.

Gamma linolenic acid (GLA) is a fatty acid of what is known as the *omega 6* variety, and among its best natural sources are *evening primrose oil* and *borage oil*.

Evening primrose oil has been used in various studies to look into its possible role in the treatment of eczema, and has been found to be quite effective in relieving its primary symptoms. These findings have been published in very well-respected journals, including *The Lancet*.

Inflammation and GLA

Among the purposes of the research was to understand more fully the part that EFAs play in eczema. As it turns out, it appears that in most sufferers there is inadequate activity of a family of anti-inflammatory prostaglandins such as PGE1 (the form made from GLA). These prostaglandins reduce inflammation by blocking the excessive activity of the inflammatory type, such as PGE2. It may be that people with eczema are actually deficient in the PGE1 precursors (substances that convert into PGE1), or they may have an inability to properly utilize PGE1 precursors due to a deficiency in the nutrients needed for this to occur. In any case, in clinical trials GLA from evening primrose oil successfully reduced the symptoms in many eczema sufferers, while also correcting any deficiencies in PGE1 precursors.

ZINC

The trace mineral *zinc* is the single most versatile of all vitamins or minerals. It is involved in more necessary, life-sustaining chemical processes than any other. As a result, in the event of a deficiency many body processes go awry. Unfortunately, zinc is also one of the most common deficiencies in the typical Western diet, thus quite a few people experience the effects of this in one or more ways. Zinc deficiency is one of the primary factors in countless medical disorders. Many cases of eczema are included in this group.

Zinc and Fatty Acids

There are times that an eczema sufferer may, rather than just being deficient in PGE1 precursors, have an impairment in the ability to utilize EFAs such as GLA in the first place. As mentioned above, there are certain nutrients that are needed for the conversion of GLA into PGE1; one of the primary ones is zinc. If zinc levels are too low, the person will not be able to convert GLA properly, thus the GLA will not be able to carry out its vital functions (which include controlling inflammation).

With this in mind, it is likely that supplementing zinc will be effective in improving many cases of eczema. This is in fact noted by many clinicians involved in its treatment. In addition to its role in eczema, zinc has been used successfully in clinical studies in the treatment of other skin disorders, as it plays a role in healing the skin in general. Zinc may also be helpful in reducing certain food-allergy mechanisms as it is required for the proper activity of digestive enzymes within the stomach that break down protein. Many people who are low in such enzymes are much more prone to food allergies.

QUERCETIN

Another natural substance that may be of enormous benefit in the treatment of eczema is called *quercetin*. Quercetin is classified as a *flavonoid* – that is, a family of pigment agents found in plants. Quercetin occurs naturally in many plants and in certain foods such as onions, broccoli and red cherries, but when used as a supplement therapeutically it is typically extracted from a herb called *sophora japonicas*. This provides a highly concentrated amount of quercetin which is much more likely to be helpful.

Quercetin should be of substantial value to eczema sufferers for many reasons, a few of which we can look at now.

INHIBITS INFLAMMATION. The anti-inflammatory effect of quercetin is well documented by research. It prevents the release of inflammatory agents such as histamine and leukotrienes from the mast cells, and can help to block production of inflammatory prostaglandins.

As histamine is the primary inflammatory agent involved in the eczema reaction, and leukotrienes are around a thousand times more inflammatory than even histamine, it is clear that quercetin could be very significant indeed in the control of eczema symptoms. As a bonus it also acts upon inflammatory prostaglandins, and thus would aid supplements such as those containing GLA in this respect.

ANTI-ALLERGIC. Scientific experimentation with quercetin has unlocked many valuable secrets into its unique biochemistry. Aside from the above-mentioned effects, it is able to reduce or inhibit chemicals involved in allergic reactions. One of the ways it accomplishes this is by stabilizing the mast cells in such a way that the release of histamine is inhibited. It also reduces the production of other inflammatory compounds involved in allergies. It is clear from this that allergic and inflammatory processes are very closely linked, especially where histamine is concerned.

Quercetin may not only be of value in controlling allergic eczema reactions, but also any other common manifestation of an allergy, whether induced by food or perhaps by something inhaled (e.g. pollen, grasses, dust, etc.).

ANTIOXIDANT. Quercetin's role as an antioxidant is vital to its benefits. As you may recall from Chapter 7, antioxidants help reduce or prevent the damaging effects of free radicals, including their ability to trigger inflammatory processes and directly damage the skin or prevent its healing.

STRENGTHENS COLLAGEN MATRIX. *Collagen* is a type of protein in the body that is found in vast quantities in connective tissue such as the skin. Collagen, more or less, helps to hold the skin cells together. Anything that damages the production of collagen, or the collagen itself, will affect the skin's integrity and ability to heal itself. Free radicals and certain chemicals released as a result of inflammation can easily damage collagen.

Quercetin helps to strengthen the bond between skin tissue cells and collagen. Quercetin functions particularly well in tandem with vitamin C, as vitamin C is required in order to make collagen in the first place.

SCUTELLARIA BAICALENSIS

The Chinese herb *scutellaria baicalensis* has been the subject of research that proves that it has a very potent anti-inflammatory effect. The research has confirmed that *scutellaria* flavonoids inhibit inflammation, but without any apparent side-effects even at therapeutic dosage levels.

More important to the issue of eczema is the fact that *scutellaria* also possesses a strong anti-allergic effect and has the ability to inhibit production of very potent allergy-induced inflammatory substances. In addition, like quercetin, the flavonoids contained in this herb should be very helpful in neutralizing many free radicals.

ANTIOXIDANTS

A vast amount of medical and scientific research over recent years has studied the effects of antioxidant therapy in the prevention and/or treatment of many health disorders such as cardiovascular disease, arthritis and cancer. As you know, due to the damaging effects of free radicals to the health of the skin, antioxidants may be very beneficial in eczema. The main antioxidant nutrients include:

- beta carotene
- vitamin A
- vitamin C
- vitamin E
- selenium
- l-cysteine
- zinc

Beta Carotene and Vitamin A

Two of the more important antioxidant nutrients for combating eczema are *beta carotene* and *vitamin A*. Beta carotene, a type of fat-soluble pigment in plants (flavonoids are water-soluble pigments), is one of the most potent antioxidants known to man. Each type of single nutrient antioxidant will be adept at neutralizing particular free radicals; beta carotene is especially good at dealing with a certain form that is especially devastating to the skin.

Interestingly, a primary role of beta carotene is to convert into the essential nutrient vitamin A, in the body. This conversion only occurs as the body requires it, and thus cannot produce potentially harmful levels of vitamin A, even if taken in very high quantities. Aside from beta carotene's antioxidant activity, this conversion into vitamin A is also of huge value in eczema – probably more value, in fact, than even its ability to scavenge free radicals. Vitamin A is itself one of the most important nutrients in the proper development and integrity of the skin. Vitamin A is also an antioxidant, but not as potent as beta carotene, and has been used successfully in clinical studies of the treatment of many skin disorders.

Vitamin C (Ascorbic Acid)

Vitamin C may be the best known of the micro-nutrients,

although most people probably do not associate it with being helpful for skin conditions.

Nevertheless, its benefits to the skin are enormous. For a start, as mentioned earlier, it is needed to make collagen, the primary protein in the skin. If vitamin C levels in the body are too low, the integrity of the skin can suffer in many ways, making it slow to heal and increasingly susceptible to inflammation.

As an antioxidant, vitamin C is also very effective at neutralizing various free radicals, including some of those that damage the skin. Above, we looked at the fact that vitamin C assists the antioxidant flavonoid quercetin. Well, quercetin and many other biologically active flavonoids (bioflavonoids) help to further the work of vitamin C as well – and not only in terms of their anti-oxidant effects.

Vitamin C also exhibits an anti-inflammatory effect. This action may be brought about by a few different mechanisms. Ascorbic acid helps detoxify histamine and aid its removal from the body. As you might expect, this should help shorten the duration of allergic reactions. As an antioxidant, vitamin C can reduce the activity of certain free radicals known to induce inflammation.

Vitamin E and Selenium

Two other primary antioxidant nutrients of note in eczema are *vitamin E* and the trace mineral *selenium*. Vitamin E is a very important nutrient to the health of the skin, especially in that it helps scavenge various free radicals, thus promoting healing and improving the elasticity of the skin. As these free radicals are produced from the oxidation of fats, which releases inflammatory prostaglandins and leukotrienes as well, vitamin E may inhibit these inflammatory chemicals, thus aiding in reducing the symptoms of eczema.

In this respect, selenium works in a similar way to vitamin E, although they cannot be used to substitute for one another. Their effects are synergistic, meaning that they work even better in tandem than the sum of their effects separately. Selenium also inhibits fat-derived free radicals and inhibits certain inflammatory chemicals.

DIGESTIVE ENZYMES

Improving your digestive capabilities should be one of your main priorities if you suffer from eczema. Improper digestion allows food allergy processes to occur in the first place. Incompletely digested food proteins are the most likely culprits in any allergic reaction. If the proteins contained in a particular food are completely digested then they will not be capable of causing an allergy. Deficiency or the relative inactivity of certain digestive enzymes is implicated in food allergies.

For eczema sufferers, taking supplements of digestive enzymes such as *hydrochloric acid* and *pancreatic enzymes* may be considered in order to enhance the digestion of proteins and other food components.

Hydrochloric Acid

Under optimal circumstances the body releases ample amounts of this enzyme into the stomach on demand to digest proteins. Unfortunately, many people have exceedingly low levels of this enzyme in their stomach when required. For some this deficiency will be caused by a lack of certain nutrients (such as zinc), but others will require the replacement of hydrochloric acid in the form of *betaine hydrochloride*.

IMPORTANT: Unless calculated by a qualified health practitioner, doses should begin at a low level such as between 300 and 600 mg. It must only be taken during or immediately after main meals. It should NOT be taken without the consent of your doctor if you suffer with or have a history of stomach or duodenal ulcer. If you experience any warmth or irritation after taking this enzyme, dosages should be reduced until this no longer occurs.

Pancreatic Enzymes

The pancreas releases certain enzymes into the duodenum (the first part of the small intestine) to further digestion. These enzymes (such as protease, amylase, and lipase) digest proteins, carbohydrates, and fats respectively. If you have food allergies there may be very strong justification for supplementing the pancreatic enzymes with *pancreatin*, as in such cases their supply is often inadequate to break down food proteins completely.

Pancreatin (4X) in levels of between 500 and 1,000 mg after main meals may be appropriate.

(For more information on food allergies and their treatment, you may want to consult my book *Allergies* [Thorsons, 1994] from this same series.)

ADDITIONAL HERBAL THERAPY

Although the list is far too long to discuss here in detail, there are many herbs with proven medicinal activity that could be relevant to eczema treatment. Many of them possess a strong anti-inflammatory effect, such as *scutellaria* (discussed earlier) and liquorice root (*glycyrrhiza glabra*), as well as special herbal constituents such as quercetin (from *sophora japonicas*).

Aside from the anti-inflammatory requirements, there is a pressing need to deal with the staphylococcus infection which afflicts the majority of sufferers and which greatly inhibits the healing process. This requirement is also within the remit of many herbs, such as golden seal (*hydrastis canadensis*), burdock root (*arctium lappa*) and liquorice root. Herbs such as the incredibly powerful immune stimulant echinacea (*echinacea purpurea*) may help the body to fight infections much more actively. Golden seal and liquorice also have well-documented immune-stimulating properties.

Any of the above herbs can be taken orally, such as in a capsule, or can be used as a tea, or as an anti-bacterial wash (e.g. golden seal) for the affected area. Cremes or salves made with the herb *chamomile* can be very soothing as well if applied to lesions.

Although these represent some of the most important and pertinent natural agents available as supplements, it is also important to ensure that your basic nutritional requirements are being met. These basic needs will ordinarily be increased, if anything, when suffering with a condition like eczema. Stress of any kind also intensifies the need for many nutrients. As a result, it may be advisable to consider taking a multiple vitamin and mineral formulation, preferably including the B vitamins (very important in stress tolerance) in higher potencies (e.g. at least 50 mg of most).

The following Table represents a hypothetical programme outlining the supplement recommendations that may be appropriate for dealing with eczema. These recommendations are based on medical and scientific research and utilize nutrients and herbs that are generally considered to be very safe. Should you choose to use these supplements, they can easily be found in health food stores and similar outlets specializing in natural health care.

> **PLEASE NOTE:** It is important to consult a qualified medical health practitioner before beginning this or any other health programme. This information is given merely as an example of the type of programme you might want to consider; it is NOT intended to be prescriptive in nature. The amounts of each supplement required will vary from person to person, and trial and error may be needed to find the most appropriate dosage.
>
> Children or pregnant or lactating women should not begin a programme of this (or any) sort without their doctor's supervision!

Dietary Suggestions for Eczema Sufferers
Avoid or Reduce Intake of

- dairy products
- wheat
- fried foods and hydrogenated fats
- alcohol
- tobacco
- caffeine
- refined sugar
- red meat
- any foods you are allergic to.

Supplement Recommendations (adult dosages)

- GLA (from evening primrose oil or borage oil): 300–600 milligrams (mg) per day (GLA potency/not that of oil; equivalent to approximately 3,000–6,000 mg of evening primrose oil).

- quercetin: 250–1,000 mg per day (preferably between meals). Quercetin is frequently found in supplements along with vitamin C and bromelain – an enzyme derived from pineapples (both of which appear to enhance the activity of quercetin).
- antioxidants:
  zinc (as picolinate, amino acid chelate or citrate): 20–40 mg per day (to be reduced to 20–30 per day once the condition is under control).

BETA CAROTENE: 15 mg per day. This amount may fulfil the requirement for vitamin A as well, although some sufferers may achieve better results by using both. If both are used, vitamin A may be suitable in levels of around 10,000 international units (iu) per day (adult dosage).

VITAMIN C: 500–1,500 mg per day. Buffered (non-acidic) vitamin C is suggested if you are prone to loose stools when taking high doses. As vitamin C is considered virtually non-toxic, there is great flexibility in dosage levels. For the best results, divide the dosage (250–750 mg twice per day), rather than taking the daily amount all at one time.

VITAMIN E (NATURAL): 400 iu per day.

SELENIUM (ORGANIC/AS SELENO-METHIONINE): 200 micrograms (mcg) per day. (The above antioxidants are available in combinations, although typically in lower dosages.)

- burdock root (*arctium lappa*): 500–1,500 mg per day.

Optional
- *scutellaria baicalensis*: 1,000–2,000 mg per day (can be

reduced once some consistent control over the condition has been achieved).

- digestive enzymes (pancreatin and betaine hydrochloride): *see pages 72–3.*
- multiple vitamin/mineral (with minimum 50 mg B-complex): as directed on label.

CHAPTER 9

Nutritional and Herbal Therapy for Psoriasis

Psoriasis is a perfect example of what is known as a multi-factorial health disorder, which simply means that it is difficult to ascertain its possible causes in a particular individual. Whereas eczema is clearly connected with allergies, there is no such obvious culprit in the case of psoriasis. Nevertheless, sufferers can centre their concentration on re-balancing the ratio between cyclic AMP and GMP (see Chapter 5), as this will prevent excessive replication of the skin cells in the first place.

It may help to recap the primary factors which can play a role in the imbalance of cAMP and cGMP, and thus the development of the symptoms of psoriasis:

- endotoxins (derived from bacterial cell walls)
- polyamines (from bacterial breakdown of amino acids in the intestine)
- the yeast/fungus *candida albicans*
- free radicals
- food allergen/antibody complexes.

Ensuring that your liver is functioning properly is a vital step you can take to eradicate the problems caused by the agents listed above. This goal can be reached with the help of various natural substances, some which will be discussed in this chapter.

As with eczema, inflammation of the skin plays a part in psoriasis. Although the inflammatory reaction may not seem as acute as in cases of eczema, the redness and much of the irritation will have a link to inflammatory compounds such as certain prostaglandins and leukotrienes.

FISH OILS

It has been discovered through published clinical studies that a particular substance derived from the oil of certain types of fatty fish is very effective in the treatment of psoriasis.

This substance is known as *eicosapentaenoic acid (EPA)* and is an *omega 3 fatty acid*. Its best natural sources are:

- salmon
- mackerel
- herring
- and various other fatty fish.

A vegetarian source of omega 3 fatty acids is linseed (flaxseed) oil.

You may remember that a certain prostaglandin called PGE2 is one of the primary chemicals responsible for producing inflammation. It is manufactured from the fatty acid arachidonic acid, which is found in animal fats. The fatty acid EPA actually converts into a prostaglandin of the PG3 series. This type of prostaglandin possesses an *anti*-inflammatory effect, as it blocks excessive production of PGE2. This is why EPA can help, just as GLA (gamma linolenic acid) can help eczema (see Chapter 8).

The amounts used in the studies were quite high, and as such would be rather expensive if the equivalent amount were taken in supplement form. You can instead choose to take only moderate levels of supplements and eat ⅓ lb of fresh salmon, mackerel or other fatty fish (preferably lightly steamed or poached) as well. If you cannot stomach the idea of eating fish every day, then on the days when you do not eat it you should probably consider increasing the level of supplemental EPA.

ANTIOXIDANTS

Antioxidants have been the subject of a great deal of medical and scientific research centred on their ability to prevent and/or treat a vast range of health disorders including cardiovascular disease, arthritis and cancer. As free radicals can be quite damaging in the case of psoriasis, you should definitely think about supplementing some of these antioxidant nutrients:

- beta carotene
- vitamin A
- vitamin C
- vitamin E
- selenium
- l-cysteine
- zinc.

All the antioxidants in this list are capable of neutralizing or playing a major part in neutralizing specific types of free radicals, known instigators of cAMP and GMP imbalances and inflammatory effects. Although all of them can be of great benefit, we will concentrate on a few of the most important ones for psoriasis sufferers.

Vitamin A

Without question, one of the more critical is the fat-soluble nutrient, *vitamin A*. Aside from its antioxidant effects, one of the most important functions of this vitamin is that it helps to maintain the general health of the skin.

If levels of vitamin A in the body are too low, the skin can change in various ways, many of which are common symptoms of a whole host of skin conditions such as psoriasis, eczema, acne and so on. Where psoriasis is concerned, aside from helping to normalize the integrity of the skin, vitamin A is known to help block the production of polyamines, which can in turn help to balance cAMP and GMP levels.

Zinc

Another of the more important antioxidant skin nutrients is the trace mineral, *zinc*. It not only aids the skin's healing processes, but also displays some anti-inflammatory capabilities (although not in the same class as EPA). Zinc is the single most versatile of all vitamins and minerals in that it is needed for more chemical processes than any other. If zinc is deficient, many health problems can arise. Zinc deficiency is, however, one of the most common in the typical Western diet.

Research has pinpointed a zinc imbalance as directly connected to psoriasis. This imbalance is related to another trace mineral, copper. Psoriasis sufferers appear typically to have too little zinc in proportion to copper; zinc supplementation may be the most appropriate way to correct this.

L-cysteine

The antioxidant *l-cysteine*, an amino acid (derivative of protein) containing sulphur, also can be very useful for treating and/or preventing psoriasis.

It is known that one of the primary sites where l-cysteine is so protective is in the liver. It is known to neutralize various liver-damaging compounds and, as a result, deserves a place in most any anti-psoriasis programme. The stronger your liver, the more effective it will be at dealing with the toxins known to trigger psoriasis.

L-cysteine is capable of direct action on skin cell proliferation as well. It is able to reduce levels of cyclic GMP, which causes an increased rate of skin cell replication. In addition, the fact that l-cysteine contains sulphur is significant because sulphur plays an important role in the integrity of the skin in general.

Vitamin E and Selenium

Vitamin E and the trace mineral *selenium* also possess powerful neutralizing effects on the various free radicals that can damage skin directly, and on those which can initiate inflammation. Vitamin E inhibits inflammatory prostaglandins and leukotrienes, which are produced from the oxidation of fats. Vitamin E is well known for promoting healing.

Selenium has some similar antioxidant effects to vitamin E, and the two are *synergistic*, which means that the effects they achieve together are actually stronger than the sum of their effects separately.

Vitamin C (Ascorbic Acid)

Vitamin C, probably the best known micro-nutrient, has many benefits to offer skin disorders. It is required to manufacture collagen, the primary protein in the body and an essential substance for 'holding the skin cells together', so to speak. A reduction in the synthesis of collagen leads to defects in the integrity of the skin.

Vitamin C is a primary antioxidant nutrient and, as such, is very effective at neutralizing free radicals, including some of those which are known to damage the skin.

An anti-inflammatory effect is also exhibited by ascorbic acid, and this would be of obvious value to anyone with psoriasis. One of its specific actions is to detoxify histamine and aid its removal from the body. As you might expect, this should help shorten the duration of inflammatory and allergic reactions. Its antioxidant activity can also help to reduce the inflammation initiated by certain free radicals.

MILK THISTLE

As with so many health problems, a great deal of published medical and scientific research has confirmed remarkable results when certain members of the herbal kingdom are used. The vast majority of this research also shows that many of these herbs offer their benefits without side-effects or toxicity, even when taken in very high dosages.

One such example of the incredible therapeutic scope of a herb in the treatment of factors related to psoriasis is milk thistle (*silybum marianum*). Its beneficial properties have been attributed to its primary active constituent, *silymarin*.

Milk Thistle and the Liver

An impressive body of evidence shows that the part of the body which seems to benefit especially from silymarin is the liver.

First of all, silymarin is known to protect the liver from incredibly potent and destructive agents, many of which are known to do horrendous damage. These agents are certain highly toxic free radicals, and the by-products of fat oxidation such as leukotrienes.

Yet another source of liver damage are the agents derived from alcohol ingestion. Milk thistle is known to protect against this type of toxicity as well. Of course, this is particularly appropriate in the case of psoriasis because, as you will know by now, alcohol can greatly exacerbate this condition.

As if this weren't enough, silymarin has also been discovered to stimulate the synthesis of protein in the liver, which leads to an increased production of healthy liver cells to replace those which have been damaged. This would be especially crucial in cases where long-term liver damage has already been incurred. As a matter of fact, research has shown that silymarin is effective in treating various liver disorders such as chronic hepatitis, cirrhosis and alcohol-induced liver defects (e.g. fatty infiltration).

All of these effects provide the greatest justification for using milk thistle in the fight against psoriasis. As mentioned earlier, it is primarily the liver that detoxifies agents known to cause psoriasis. For most psoriasis sufferers, this detoxification is not happening effectively enough, whether due to a weakened liver or unusually high levels of exposure to the damaging agents (e.g. bacterial toxins, polyamines, free radicals, candida albicans, allergen/antibody complexes, etc.). So anything that can help the liver get its job done is to be recommended.

Milk Thistle and Inflammation

Silymarin neutralizes leukotrienes by preventing their production. High leukotriene levels are noted in people with psoriasis, so again, taking milk thistle would be advisable.

ADDITIONAL HERBAL THERAPY

There are several herbs whose properties would seem to make them beneficial for psoriasis sufferers. Golden seal (*hydrastis canadensis*) and sarsaparilla root (*smilax* spp.) are two examples which have been scientifically proven to be of value either in correcting some of the primary causes or in treating psoriasis itself.

Golden Seal

Golden seal has several benefits confirmed by scientific studies, many of which relate to its anti-bacterial and anti-fungal activity. It also is known to be capable of detoxifying the liver.

As many of the problems associated with psoriasis appear to begin with bacteria-derived agents, anything that helps to kill harmful bacteria is a bonus. Golden seal also kills candida albicans. An added benefit is that it is known to inhibit the production of polyamines, of course, toxins which disturb the ratio between cAMP and cGMP.

Sarsaparilla Root

This herb has a long history of traditional use in the treatment of various skin complaints. In the case of psoriasis, this herb's reputation has been confirmed by clinical research. Its beneficial effect may be due to the fact that it appears to aid in the removal of bacterial cell-wall constituents known to alter cAMP:cGMP ratios.

DIGESTIVE ENZYMES

As polyamines are clearly one of the more prominent factors in the development of psoriasis, inhibiting them is obviously important. They can be produced if either the dietary protein is inadequately digested and/or if amino acids from protein remain in the intestines too long without being properly absorbed. Improper digestion of protein is also a major cause of food allergies, which are also known to be potential triggers of psoriasis.

A deficiency of or lack of activity on the part of certain protein-digesting enzymes will mean that proteins are not digested completely. In such cases, replacing these enzymes can be of great help.

Hydrochloric Acid

Hydrochloric acid is the primary protein-digesting enzyme in the stomach. When digestion is strong, the body releases adequate amounts of this enzyme into the stomach on demand to digest proteins. Unfortunately, many people do not have adequate levels of this enzyme to deal with the quantity of protein being consumed. This deficit can occur due to a lack of certain nutrients such as zinc, however many people may require the supplemental replacement of hydrochloric acid in the form called *betaine hydrochloride*.

IMPORTANT: Unless calculated by a qualified health practitioner, doses should begin at a low level such as between 300 and 600 mg. It must be taken during or immediately after major meals; it should NOT be taken without the consent of a doctor if you suffer with or have a history of stomach or duodenal ulcers. If you experience any undue warmth or irritation after taking this enzyme, dosages should be reduced until this no longer occurs.

Pancreatic Enzymes

Certain enzymes are released from the pancreas into the duodenum (the first part of the small intestine) to further digestion. There are three main classifications of pancreatic enzymes, one of which (*protease*) is responsible for furthering the digestion of protein. As with hydrochloric acid, there can be inadequate activity on the part of the protease enzymes; thus you may benefit from replacing pancreatic enzymes with the supplement known as *pancreatin*. An appropriate level may be between 500 and 1,000 mg of pancreatin (4X) after main meals.

The use of the above enzymes may significantly help to reduce the risk of digesting food proteins incompletely, to prevent the build-up of polyamines and the onset of food allergies.

SOLUBLE FIBRE

In Chapter 7 we looked at the role of dietary fibre in aiding the removal of waste from the intestines. The retention of intestinal waste gives rise to many types of harmful toxins, such as polyamines. Also, if such removal is slow there is more opportunity for harmful bacteria (and bacterial components), candida albicans, and so on to do their damage. Keeping these harmful agents from proliferating would be a clear advantage not only in fighting psoriasis, but also in improving your general state of health.

Soluble fibre is particularly suitable for removing intestinal toxins. As you may remember, this is the type that can absorb water, and as such can also absorb moisture-borne toxins in the intestines. Soluble fibre softens as well, and thus can be more soothing to a weakened or sensitive intestinal wall.

The natural therapies that have been described are some of the most important and heavily researched in the treatment of psoriasis symptoms and/or its causes. At the same time, however, it is important to ensure that your general nutritional requirements are being met. Such basic needs are often increased when a person is suffering with a health disorder such as psoriasis. As stress may make matters worse, basic supplementation should also include those nutrients which stressed individuals need. To supplement your food intake, it may be advisable therefore to consider a multiple vitamin and mineral formulation, preferably including the B vitamins (important in stress control) in higher potencies (e.g. at least 50 mg of most).

ULTRAVIOLET LIGHT

Research has also shown that exposure to ultraviolet (UV) light is very helpful in psoriasis therapy, as it reduces excessive replication of the skin cells. Although sunshine is a good way to get ultraviolet A and B rays, exposure to UVB lamps seems to provide adequate benefits without as high a risk of side-effects as exposure to UVA.

The following Table represents a hypothetical programme which outlines the supplement recommendations that may be appropriate for a successful psoriasis programme. These recommendations are based on medical and scientific research and utilize nutrients and herbs which are considered to be very safe. Should you choose to use such supplements, they can be found in health food stores and similar outlets specializing in natural health care.

Dietary Suggestions for Psoriasis Sufferers
Avoid or Reduce Intake of
- alcohol
- fried foods and hydrogenated fats

> **PLEASE NOTE:** It is important to consult a qualified medical health practitioner before beginning this or any other health programme. This information is given merely as an example of the type of programme you might want to consider; it is NOT intended to be prescriptive in nature. The amounts of each supplement required will vary from person to person, and trial and error may be needed to find the most appropriate dosage.
>
> Children or pregnant or lactating women should not begin a programme of this (or any) sort without their doctor's supervision!

- tobacco
- caffeine
- refined sugar
- red meat
- dairy products (unless skimmed – but none at all if allergic)
- any foods you are allergic to.

Recommendations (adult dosages)
- EPA (potency given here is not that of the fish oil itself, but of the EPA): 350–1,000 milligrams (mg) per day (do NOT take without medical consent if using prescription anticoagulants such as warfarin).
- antioxidants:

ZINC (AS PICOLINATE, AMINO ACID CHELATE OR CITRATE): 20–30 mg per day.

VITAMIN A: 10,000–15,000 international units (iu) per day (adult dosage – NOT for pregnant/lactating women).

High dosages may be required by some people; if so, this should be monitored by a physician.

L-CYSTEINE: 250–500 mg per day.

VITAMIN E (NATURAL): 400 iu per day

SELENIUM (ORGANIC/AS SELENO-METHIONINE): 200 micrograms (mcg) per day.

VITAMIN C: 500–1,500 mg per day. Buffered (non-acidic) vitamin C is suggested if you are prone to loose stools when taking high doses. As vitamin C is considered virtually non-toxic, there is great flexibility in dosage levels. For the best results, divide the dosage (250–750 mg twice per day), rather than taking the daily amount all at one time. (The above antioxidants are available in combinations, although typically in lower dosages.)

- milk thistle (*silybum marianum*): 70–210 mg of silymarin per day. The proper dosage should not be based strictly on the potency of the milk thistle itself, but rather on the amount of silymarin.
- sarsaparilla root (*smilax* spp.): 500–1,500 mg per day.

Optional
- psyllium husks (soluble fibre): 2,000–4,000 mg per day (in divided doses and with full glass of water).
- digestive enzymes (pancreatin and betaine hydrochloride): *see pages 86–7*.
- golden seal (*hydrastis canadensis*): 500 mg per day
- multiple vitamin/mineral (with minimum 50 mg B-complex): as directed on label.

REFERENCES

Allison, J., *Southern Medical Journal* 38 (1945), pp.235–41

Atherton, D., *et al.*, *Lancet* i (1978), p.401

Ayers, S., *Archives Dermatol. Syphilol.* 20 (1929), pp.854–9

Bittiner, S., *et al.*, *Lancet* i (1988), pp.378–80

Boer, J., *et al.*, *Arch. Dermatology* 120 (1984), pp.52–7

British Medical Association, *Guide to Medicines and Drugs* (Dorling Kindersley, 1991)

Buckley, R., *Journal of the American Medical Association* 248 (1982), p.2627

Bulkley, L., *Journal of the American Medical Association* 59 (1912), p.535

Clemenson, C., *Journal of Nutrition* 110/4 (1980), pp.662–8

Commings, W. and Williams, E., *Gut* 19 (1978), p.715

Dockhorn, R. and Smith, T., *Annals of Allergy* 47 (1981), pp.264–6

Evans, F., *British Journal of Clinical Practice* 12 (1958), pp.269–74

Finn, R., *et al.*, *Clinical Ecology* 3/3 (1985), pp.129–31

Foreman, J. (ed.), *Journal of Allergy and Clinical Immunology* 73 (1984), pp.769–74

Gerrard, J., *et al.*, *Annals of Allergy* 36 (1976), p.10

Grosch, W. and Laskawy, G., *Biochem. Biophys. Acta* 575 (1979), pp.439–45

Hikino, H., *et al.*, *Planta Medica* 50 (1984), pp.248–50

Innerfield, I., *Enzymes in Clinical Medicine* (New York: McGraw-Hill, 1960)

Jacobs, A., *Paediatr. Ann.* 5 (1976), pp.763–71

Jordan, J. and Whitlock, F., *British Journal of Dermatology* 86 (1972), pp.574–84

Journal of Investigative Dermatology 81 (1983), pp.385–7

Juhlin, L. and Vahlquist, C., *British Journal of Dermatology* 108 (1983), pp.33–7

Juhlin, L., *et al.*, *Acta Derm. Venereol.* (Stockholm) 62 (1982), pp.211–14

Kamimura, M., *Journal of Vitaminology* 18/4 (1972), p.204

Katayama, H. and Hori, H., *Acta Dermatol. Venereol.* (Stockholm) 64 (1984), pp.1–4

Kettler, A., *et al.*, *Journal of the American Academy of Dermatology* 18/6 (1988), pp.1267–73

Kimura, Y., *et al.*, *Planta Medica* 54 (1985), pp.132–6

Kubo, M., *et al.*, *Chem. Pharm. Bulletin* 32 (1984), pp.2724–9

Kuwano, S. and Yamauchi, K., *Chem. Pharm. Bull.* 8 (1960), pp.491–6

Lee, C., *et al.*, *Archives of Otolaryngology* 90 (1969), p.113

Leung, R., *British Journal of Dermatology* 123/3 (1990), pp.319–23

Lithell, H., *et al.*, *Acta Derm. Venereol.* (Stockholm) 63/5 (1983), pp.397–403

McCarty, N., *Medical Hypothesis* 13 (1984), pp.45–50

McGovern, J. J., *Annals of Allergy* 44 (1980), p.57

Majewski, S., *et al.*, *Arch. Dermatol. Research* 280 (1989), pp.499–501

Manku, M., *et al.*, *Prostaglandins, Leukotrienes and Medicine* 9 (1982), pp.615–28

Michaelsson, G. and Ljunghall, K., *Acta Derm. Venereol.* 70/4 (1990), pp.304–8

Middleton, E. and Drzewiecki, G., *International Archives of Allergy and Applied*

Immunology 77 (1985),
pp.155–7

Monk, B. and Neill, S.,
Dermatologica 173/2
(1986), pp.57–60

Morse, P., *et al.*, British
Journal of Dermatology 121
(1989), pp.75–90

Murray, M. and Pizzorno, J.,
*Encyclopaedia of Natural
Medicine* (Macdonald and
Co., 1990)

Nasr, S., *et al.*, *Journal of
Affective Disease* 3 (1981),
p.291

Nutrition Foundation, *Present
Knowledge in Nutrition*
(Washington, DC: 5th
edn, 1984)

Paganelli, R., *et al.*, *Lancet* i
(1979), p.1270

Parish, P., *Medical Treatments:
The Benefits and Risks*
(Penguin, 1991)

Passmore, R. and Eastwood,
M., *Human Nutrition and
Dietetics* (Edinburgh:
Churchill Livingstone,
1986)

Pearce, F., *et al.*, *Journal of
Allergy and Clinical
Immunology* 73 (1984),
pp.819–23

Pekarek, R., *et al.*, *American*

Journal of Clinical Nutrition
32 (1979), p.1466

Podell, R., *Clinical Ecology* 3/2
(1985), pp.79–84

Poikolainen, K., *et al.*, British
Medical Journal 300
(1990), pp.780–3

Proctor, M., *et al.*, Arch.
Dermatology 115 (1979),
pp.945–9

Rainsford, K., *et al.*, *Agents
and Actions* supp. 8 (1981),
pp.164–72

Ransberger, K., *Arthritis and
Rheumatism* 8 (1986),
pp.16–19

Rao, M. and Field, M.,
Biochem. Soc. Trans. 12
(1984), pp.177–80

Reinhardt, M. C., *Journal of
Allergy* 53 (1984), p.597

Rinkel, H., *Journal of
Pediatrics* 32 (1948), p.266

Rinkel, H., *et al.*, *Archives of
Otolaryngology* 79 (1964),
p.71

Robbins, S. and Cotran, R.,
Pathological Basis of Disease
(Philadelphia, PA: W. B.
Saunders and Co., 1979)

Rosenberg, E. and Belew, P.,
Arch. Dermatology 118
(1982), pp.1434–44

Rowe, A. H. and Rowe, A.,

Food Allergy: Its Manifestation and Control and Elimination Diets (Springfield, IL: C. C. Thomas, 1972)

Salmi, H. and Sarna, S., *Scandinavian Journal of Gastroenterology* 17 (1982), pp.517–21

Sampson, H., *Journal of Allergy and Clinical Immunology* 71 (1983), pp.473–80

Schauff, C., *et al.*, *Human Physiology* (St. Louis, MO: Time Mirror/Mosby College, 1990)

Selye, H., *Stress in Health and Disease* (Butterworths, 1976)

Seville, R., *British Journal of Dermatology* 97 (1977), p.297

Siccardi, A., *et al.*, *Infect. Immunology* 33 (1981), pp.710–13

Soter, N. and Baden, H., *Pathophysiology of Dermatologic Disease* (New York: McGraw-Hill, 1984)

Strosser, A. and Nelson, L., *Annals of Allergy* 10 (1952), pp.703–4

Thurman, F., *New England Journal of Medicine* 227 (1942), pp.128–33

Trevino, R. J., *Laryngoscope* 91 (1981), p.1913

Vorhees, J. and Duell, E., *Adv. in Cyclic Nucleotide Res.* 5 (1975), pp.755–7

Weber, G. and Galle, K., *Med Welt* 34 (1983), pp.108–11

Werbach, M., *Nutritional Influences on Illness* (Thorsons, 1987)

White, A., *et al.*, *Arch. Dermatology* 119 (1983), pp.541–7

Wright, S., *Journal of Nutritional Medicine* 1 (1990), pp.301–13

Wright, S., *et al.*, *British Journal of Nutrition* 62/3 (1989), pp.693–8

Yashimoto, T., *et al.*, *Biochem. Biophys. Res. Commun.* 116 (1983), pp.612–18